JOURNEY TO YOU

A STEP-BY-STEP GUIDE TO BECOMING WHO YOU WERE BORN TO BE

BY STEVE OLSHER

This book is designed to provide general information regarding the subject matter covered. The author has taken reasonable precautions in the preparation of this material and believes the facts presented in the book are accurate as of the time of writing. However, neither the author nor the publisher assumes any responsibility for any errors or omissions. The author and publisher disclaim any liability resulting from the use or application of the information contained in this book. The information is not intended to serve as professional advice related to individual situations.

Bold Press books may be purchased for educational, business, or sales promotional use. For information, please write: Special Markets Department, Bold Press, 5940 W. Touhy Avenue #190, Niles, IL 60714.

ISBN: 978-0-9844796-0-3

For free templates and further information, please visit www.SteveOlsher.com.

Trademarks of Steve Olsher are not designated in the text of this book. The following are trademarks of Steve Olsher and may not be used without permission:

The Vortex of Vulnerability™
The Vortex of Invincibility™
Circle of Four™
The Pinnacle Pyramid™
The S.L.A.P.™ (The Seven Life-Altering Principles)
YāNo™
The Sufficiency Theory™
The Pre-Sent Future™
The Vitality Curve™
What Is Your *WHAT*?™
The Seven Seeds of Your Soul™
Hone It to Own It!™
The destination *is* the road. The *journey* is the destination.™

ACKNOWLEDGMENTS

There are many people I would like to thank for supporting me in my journey: Preston and Emily, for your gift that will never be forgotten. Jim, for your unwavering inspiration. Alan, for encouraging me to put pen to paper. Robin and Symeon, for your brilliant ideas and thoughts. Mom, Al, Sylvia, Irv, Dad, and Barb (who created the visuals for The Pinnacle Pyramid, The Vitality Curve, The Coat of Arms, The Circle of Four, and did an incredible job of formatting), for helping to make me the man that I am. Gerry, for creating the visual for The Pre-Sent Future. Rania El-Sorrogy, for designing the Pinnacle Pyramid. Hy Bender, Mary Mihaly, and Lisbeth Levine (who edited this book), for teaching me the difference between writing and being a writer. Bobby, Isaiah, and Xavier, for helping me to recognize that love truly knows no bounds. And Lena, the love of my life, who makes the world a better place to be, and who always keeps me on point with her guidance, support, and compassion.

I love and appreciate each of you and could not have completed this without you. You forever have my gratitude.

CONTENTS

INTRODUCTION   1

PART I: ESTABLISH THE FOUNDATION

CHAPTER 1: INTRODUCTION TO THE FOUR STAGES OF LEARNING   9

CHAPTER 2: THE VORTEX OF VULNERABILITY   17

CHAPTER 3: THE VORTEX OF INVINCIBILITY   33

CHAPTER 4: THE NEXT STAGES OF LEARNING   49

CHAPTER 5: THE PINNACLE   59

PART II: REALIZE PERMANENT, POSITIVE CHANGE

CHAPTER 6: THE SEVEN LIFE-ALTERING PRINCIPLES (THE S.L.A.P.)   83

CHAPTER 7: YĀNO   89

CHAPTER 8: RECLAIM THE CANYON   97

CHAPTER 9: THE SUFFICIENCY THEORY   105

CHAPTER 10: RETRAIN YOUR BRAIN   117

CHAPTER 11: THE ALTAR OF JACK'S CATHEDRAL   131

CHAPTER 12: THE NOT-SO-GOLDEN RULE   145

CHAPTER 13: THE SLOW DEATH OF NOT BEING THE STAR   153

PART III: BECOME WHO YOU WERE BORN TO BE

CHAPTER 14: WHAT IS YOUR *WHAT?* AN INTRODUCTION   165

CHAPTER 15: THE THREE-STEP PROCESS OF IDENTIFYING YOUR *WHAT*   173

CHAPTER 16: NOW THAT YOU'VE FOUND YOUR *WHAT...* NOW WHAT?!   195

PART IV: FORGE YOUR PATH—CREATE YOUR LEGACY

CHAPTER 17: PUTTING IT ALL TOGETHER   207

CHAPTER 18: WRITING YOUR LETTER OF REFLECTION   219

CHAPTER 19: A FINAL WORD   225

NOTES   231

ABOUT THE AUTHOR   237

INTRODUCTION

Success means having the courage, the determination, and the will to become the person you were meant to be.

—George Sheehan, Physician and Author, 1918-1993

Have you ever wondered why we so dearly love the story of Cinderella, the downtrodden servant who becomes a princess? Or the tale of Luke Skywalker, a humble farm boy who becomes the savior of the galaxy?

If you think deeply about their stories, you'll realize that while each undergoes an incredible transformation, neither emerges as an entirely different, new person.

Instead, they start out with their inherent greatness suppressed by difficult childhoods and buried by harsh circumstances. Over the course of their adventures, however, they learn to shed the shackles of their past and become their true selves—glorious leaders and heroes.

The central message of these stories has great resonance for all of us. As we endure life's hardships, we tend to lose touch with our inner greatness. We start to make distasteful compromises, settle for less, and become detached from our deepest selves.

JOURNEY TO YOU empowers you to follow the examples of Cinderella and Luke. By discovering your true potential, you'll become who you were born to be and achieve profound success and fulfillment.

This will benefit not only you, but the lives of everyone around you. Once you shed your skin and dump your baggage, you'll possess the magic to positively affect an astonishing number of people.

A LITTLE ABOUT ME

I grew up in Evanston, Illinois—a child of modest beginnings. My parents divorced when I was seven, and I lived with my mom, who did her best to raise me, my brother, and sister on a limited income.

I started working at age 10. Odd jobs, shoveling snow, raking leaves, mowing lawns. You name it—if it paid I was there.

High School Graduation Picture

In high school, I had a 4.0 GPA. We're not talking Grade Point Average—we're talking Girls Per Attempt. In other words, for every 10 girls I asked out, I averaged about four dates.

Not bad for a short, wannabe player with a frizzy mullet and a gold hoop earring. During high school I waited tables, pumped gas, fixed cars, stocked shelves, and worked in restaurants. During my freshman year of college, I began to DJ and eventually became good enough to spin in the clubs throughout Illinois.

This led to my sharing the stage with some of the biggest DJs in the late '80s and early '90s, including Bad Boy Bill and Julian Jumpin' Perez.

At 20, I opened The Funky Pickle! on the main drag in Carbondale, Illinois, just off the campus of Southern Illinois University. The Pickle was a unique concept—a non-alcohol nightclub smack dab in the middle of Carbondale's alcohol-suffused nightlife. At first glance, you would think I was making a huge mistake. But I had a plan.

I knew the local teenagers had very few options for entertainment. So from 8-11:30 p.m., we catered to those under the age of 18. We became very popular, very quickly.

At 11:30, we closed, cleaned the place up, and re-opened at midnight. From midnight on (often until 5 or 6 a.m.) we catered to those 18 and over.

By city ordinance, bars that served alcohol had to close at 1:30 a.m. Given that we didn't have a liquor license, we could stay open all night long—and we had plenty of takers.

Ultimately I had a falling out with my business partner, but my entrepreneurial fire was now fully ablaze. I've since gone on to build multiple businesses ranging from music to real estate to pioneering online stores and have applied a creative slant to each endeavor.

While not all have proven successful, I've had the pleasure of learning from and working with people from all walks of life. I've also experienced monumental ups and downs along the way. I've gone through divorce and business failure, financial ruin and battles with depression; I've fallen in love, had children, and built successful businesses. In short, I've seen it all.

I've been married to my wife Lena since 1997 and have three incredible sons. Nothing teaches you more about life than love.

Love requires patience, kindness and selflessness—traits that don't always come naturally to me. Therefore, I work at it everyday. And while I often make mistakes, the look of disappointment in the eyes of someone I love always brings me back to center.

Since August 2000, I've trained in Brazilian Jiu-Jitsu under one of its true Grandmasters—Carlson Gracie Jr.—and trained under the late Carlson Gracie Sr. Junior is a legend in the sport, having won 10 Brazilian Jiu-Jitsu championships, and is a member of the family that put Brazilian Jiu-Jitsu on the map.

If you're unfamiliar with Jiu-Jitsu, it's a ground-fighting technique where the objective is to force your opponent to "give-up." This subtle persuasion takes place as a result of chokes or limb manipulation (think broken arms, legs, ankles, elbows, etc.).

Being choked to the point of unconsciousness and having limbs twisted in directions you never thought humanly possible has resulted in my learning humility and respect in the most painful of ways.

These life experiences serve as the foundation for this book's bluntly honest, cut-to-the-chase perspectives about personal reinvention.

PLEASE TAKE THE SHORTCUT

I wrote *JOURNEY TO YOU* because I want you to celebrate the gifts that are uniquely yours, share your special talents with the world, and become who you were born to be. Upon completion, you'll have a clear understanding of your life's purpose—and be fired up about, and highly focused on, achieving it.

I'm a steadfast believer that we should learn from the trials and tribulations of those selfless enough to teach. I've been fortunate to benefit from the guidance of incredible mentors—I hope you'll allow me to mentor you.

Over the past 20 years, I've developed and refined the proprietary exercises, theories, and principles you'll find in these pages. Each is crafted from my own often painful, hands-on experience.

I've made the mistakes and suffered the inevitable results. You don't have to.

My unique methodology blends ancient wisdom from a multitude of spiritual leaders, including Buddha, with revolutionary lessons from modern theorists, such as Dr. Thomas Gordon, creator of *The Four Stages of Learning*. These teachings, combined with my unique exercises and singular approach to realizing permanent, positive change, form a proven system for ultimate achievement.

As creator and facilitator of The Reinvention Workshop, I've witnessed my participants' amazing transformations using this system. You'll meet some of them in upcoming chapters as they share key steps in their journeys.

The tools I provide show you powerful shortcuts you can immediately implement to create the life you deserve and desire while avoiding the pitfalls of going it alone. As Jim Rohn, the author and motivational speaker largely credited with launching the careers of Tony Robbins, Mark Victor Hansen, Jack Canfield, and others, aptly put it, however: "You can't hire someone else to do your push-ups for you." To create your ideal life, you must be willing to do the work.

How This Book is Organized

Journey To You is organized into four parts:

Part I enables you to Establish The Foundation and demonstrates how The Four Stages of Learning impacts who you are and why you do what you do. You'll learn how to set deep anchors into your soul that empower you to avoid being a windsock, constantly blown off path by the whims of others. And you'll tap into your formidable inner-strength and learn to master areas of your life to such an extent that you'll appear magical to the rest of the world.

Part II teaches you how to Realize Permanent, Positive Change and introduces you to *The Seven Life-Altering Principles (The S.L.A.P.).* Each principle provides powerful life strategies and helps you establish clear guidelines for living with conviction and purpose.

Part III guides you to Become Who You Were Born to Be by answering the key question—*What Is Your WHAT?* Your *WHAT* is the one vocation you're compelled to pursue. It's not something you've chosen, but that which has chosen you. Living within the framework of this distinction will help you experience freedom and self-expression unlike anything you've ever known.

You'll also be introduced to *The Seven Seeds of Your Soul* and perform exercises that support the vigorous pursuit of your *WHAT*.

Part IV brings all the elements of your reinvention together and encourages you to Forge Your Path and Create Your Legacy. You'll take on the life-focusing exercises of constructing your *Coat of Arms,* writing your *Letter of Reflection,* and completing *My Journey*—three easy-to-use references that provide a clear understanding of who you are, what you were born to do, and the objectives you've identified for your life.

WHAT YOU WILL ACCOMPLISH

Completing JOURNEY TO YOU empowers you to:
- Reconnect with who you really are.
- Leverage your natural talents, honing in on the key areas where you're wired to succeed.
- Uncover and eliminate barriers you've unconsciously created.
- Achieve fundamental change at the deepest level of your being—change that will embed within you and become inseparable from your thoughts and actions.
- Identify your WHAT and establish a plan of action for achieving your natural-born greatness.
- Identify your life's purpose, goals, and the motivating factors that inspire you.

I strongly believe the destination **is** the road, and the **journey** is the destination.

JOURNEY TO YOU is a quest for the most precious of destinations: your true self. Let me guide you through it.

PART I

ESTABLISH THE FOUNDATION

CHAPTER 1

INTRODUCTION TO THE FOUR STAGES OF LEARNING

Most people live, whether physically, intellectually or morally, in a very restricted circle of their potential being. They make use of a very small portion of their possible consciousness, and of their soul's resources in general. Much like a man who, out of his whole body, should get into a habit of using and moving only his little finger. Great emergencies and crises show us how much greater our vital resources are than we had supposed.

—William James, psychologist and philosopher, May 6, 1906

What if your child was dying of a rare disease and only had six months to live? And what if you learned about a miracle antidote that cost $1 million and you only had a few thousand dollars to your name?

How hard would you bust your butt to make that million? How quickly could you turn the impossible into the definite?

Like a finely-tuned, high-performance sports car, you operate with multiple gears. Seldom, however, are you faced with crises or emergencies that require you to maximize your potential and leverage your abilities to create dynamic results.

Have you ever heard a story about a terrified mother lifting an impossibly heavy object to free her child from harm's way? Or a father who fights off a wild animal with his bare hands to protect his family?

While, hopefully, you'll never be faced with one of these situations, the fact remains that your life is governed by the self-imposed limitations you've established. Such limitations run the gamut from repeating self-defeating phrases such as "I could never do that," to maintaining destructive ways of being, such as staying at a job you loathe because you've convinced yourself that you have no other options.

> **Ultimately, the farther you can stretch these limitations, the more fulfilled you'll be.**

As William James observed, most people use a very small portion of their possible consciousness and of their body's resources in general. You hold the power to kick it into overdrive. You also hold the power to continue coasting.

What speed are you willing to travel to save someone you love? What speed are you willing to travel to save yourself?

CREATING YOUR FOUNDATION

In order to become who you were born to be you first need to understand who you are. This is essential for manifesting long-term, sustainable change that continually supports the realization of your goals and objectives.

Part I helps you create this change by identifying the cravings of your being and the restricting forces that prevent you from living the life you deserve and desire.

Few people reach their potential because they operate like a windsock—letting chance dictate their lives and moving in whatever direction the whims of others takes them.

The process of personal reinvention is too often similar to the "new-car-high" many experience. For the first few months, the love is deep. Each week, the car is washed, waxed, and vacuumed. After a period of time, however, the love fades and what was once a prized possession becomes just another car.

To remain focused and inspired to pursue living as your true self, it's imperative to set deep anchors into your soul and establish an unyielding foundation upon which to build a new, more powerful you. This will prevent you from being "enlightened" for a brief period of time and then returning to old habits.

Picture a beautiful glass and steel skyscraper built upon an unstable base. While passers-by may admire the impressive structure that reaches for the stars, a weak infrastructure below the surface will eventually send the whole building toppling to the ground.

My objective is to help you construct an unshakable footing that will support the person you'll be once you've completed this book. Without resolute grounding, you, like the poorly constructed skyscraper, will find yourself unstable in your approach to life, easily swayed by those trying to blow you off path, and continually thwarted in your desire to achieve meaningful satisfaction and contentment.

To create an extraordinary life, follow the path to freedom. This requires you to:

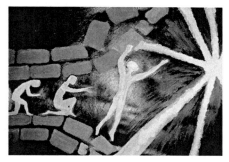

a. *Become aware of strengths and self-imposed limitations.*

b. *Make a conscious choice about what to do with these strengths and limitations.*

c. *Improve upon, maintain, modify, or eliminate them.*

One of the most effective tools for obtaining such understanding and creating the necessary blank slate for reinvention is *The Four Stages of Learning*. While very powerful, the Four Stages is a bit dry.

Please grab a glass of water and bear with me as I take you through it. I promise you'll reach the other side with a compelling new perspective on your life and the strength required to stay clear, focused, and fired up about becoming who you were born to be.

THE FOUR STAGES OF LEARNING

The discovery that there are four distinct stages of learning comes from Dr. Thomas Gordon, who in the 1970s developed the Conscious Competence Learning Stages Model. It was first published in his *Teacher Effectiveness Training Instructor Guide* and is widely used in academia and business to this day.

Behind this bland, academic title lies the key to understanding why you're able to excel in certain aspects of your life and lag in others.

The four stages are:

1. **Unconscious Incompetence:** Not knowing what your strengths or problems are or how to identify them.
2. **Conscious Incompetence:** Having the ability to identify strengths or problems, but not the desire or knowledge to improve upon or correct them.
3. **Conscious Competence:** Having the proficiency to achieve your desired results, but needing to be consciously focused on your process as you perform the actions required.
4. **Unconscious Competence:** Having the proficiency to achieve your desired results without having to think about your process (a.k.a. "The Zone").

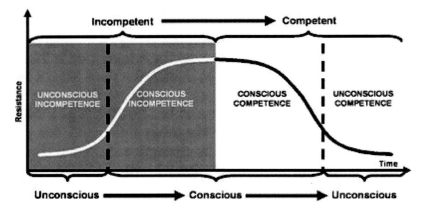

The diagram shown details Gordon's model. It illustrates how the process of learning begins at the stage of Unconscious Incompetence—exemplified by low resistance, little time expended, and a high degree of incompetence—and flows to Unconscious Competence—exemplified by low resistance and a high degree of competence with little time expended to attain one's desired results.

Ultimately, your goal is to attain the stage of Unconscious Competence in as many areas of your life as possible. Many correlate this stage with having achieved "mastery."

The world applauds and generously compensates those who have become a master of their craft. While pursuing mastery of additional skills should be your ongoing objective, mastering even one skill can result in significant spiritual and psychological benefit for both you and those you touch.

You have the ability to inspire the world. Let's look at Gordon's Four Stages model and how its revolutionary approach to understanding how we learn is an extraordinary tool you can leverage to create the results you want and shed the habits you don't.

STAGE ONE: UNCONSCIOUS INCOMPETENCE

In this stage of learning, the following characteristics are present:
- You're not aware of strengths or problems.
- You're not aware that you lack a course of action to benefit from strengths or address problems.
- You might deny the relevance of strengths or problems and/or usefulness of the strengths or missing skills.
- You must become conscious of strengths or problems, as well as your incompetence to improve upon or address them, before the process of attaining mental or physical proficiency can begin.

Put simply, in this stage of learning you're not aware of your strengths or problems, or your inability to address them.

Life in the stage of Unconscious Incompetence is exemplified by a "What's wrong with the rest of the world?" attitude. Within this unaware state, it's everyone else who doesn't "get it" and you experience frustration due to your inability to recognize personal shortcomings or strengths.

You must be ruthless with yourself to identify where you live within the state of Unconscious Incompetence and, in the next two chapters, I'll show you how. Until you're willing to do so, your life will run on autopilot and your reactions to the world will continue to be what is most familiar and most comfortable. This is a destructive pattern that eliminates the possibility for growth. And if you're not growing, you're dying.

To become aware of issues you don't realize control your quality of life, commit to exploring who you are and why you do what you do.

This will take more than simply reading. It requires periodically doing the exercises in this book.

The most effective way to approach each exercise is with an open mind and without distractions. Be brutally honest and write down exactly what comes to mind. Try not to let fear or self-sabotaging thoughts interfere with the process.

Taking on your reinvention from a place of denial, or with the concern that others are going to read through your notes and get mad at you for what you've written about them, is counter-productive. This is your private journal. Protect it as such.

> ### *Treat each exercise as if your life depends on the quality of your results. It does.*

While doing so may sometimes be difficult, it's the only way to extinguish the components of who you are that aren't serving you well. Otherwise, the "old you" will come back with a vengeance and overthrow everything you've learned. This is not an option.

The next chapter, The Vortex of Vulnerability, begins your exploration of Stage One—Unconscious Incompetence—and presents one of the most challenging exercises in this entire book.

It asks you to dig deep to identify hidden elements of your personality and underlying drivers that largely control your life.

Once you're able to recognize these mischievous sprites, you'll hold the power to either permanently eradicate them from your thoughts or continue to allow them to come along for the ride. It's time to disengage the cruise control.

INTRODUCTION TO THE FOUR STAGES OF LEARNING—TAKEAWAYS

- The farther you can stretch your self-imposed limitations, the more fulfilled you'll be.
- Most people operate like a windsock—blown about by the whims of others and never realizing their potential.
- Set deep anchors into your soul and establish an unyielding foundation upon which to build a new, more powerful you.
- Follow the path to freedom:

  a. Become aware of strengths and self-imposed limitations.

  b. Make a conscious choice about what to do with these strengths and limitations.

  c. Improve upon, maintain, modify, or eliminate them.

- The Four Stages of Learning is a powerful tool you can leverage to create the results you want and shed the habits you don't.
- The world applauds and generously compensates those who have become a master of their craft.
- Stage One is Unconscious Incompetence: You lack awareness of your strengths and problems, as well as your inability to improve upon or address them.
- You must be ruthless with yourself to identify where you live within the state of Unconscious Incompetence.
- Treat each exercise as if your life depends on the quality of your results. It does.

CHAPTER 2

THE VORTEX OF VULNERABILITY

Knowing others is intelligence; knowing yourself is true wisdom.
Mastering others is strength; mastering yourself is true power.

—Tao Te Ching, ancient Chinese spiritual text by Lao-tzu

There's an old adage that says "Better the devil you know than the devil you don't."

And it's dead wrong.

The fear of the devil you don't know is much worse than the devil you do. Positioning yourself to look what you don't know in the eye—and refusing to back down—will empower you to achieve breakthrough results.

The Vortex of Vulnerability will help cultivate this strength. It is composed of a three-step process (four if you choose to take on the Bonus Step). Each step will help you gain clarity as to who you are and why you do what you do.

When combined, the steps will help you move forward with conviction and purpose and reveal aspects of your life you aren't consciously aware of but have a profound impact on your behavior.

Let's begin.

STEP ONE

- *Identify three recent times in your life when you absolutely "lost it."*

"Losing it" varies for different people. It might mean yelling at someone at the top of your lungs, sending a nasty email, or not returning someone's phone call. The specific way in which you "lose it" isn't important for this exercise.

What matters is that you identify the times when you've lost control and resorted to your most primal, or natural, way of being. Take the time to replay these moments in your mind with as much detail as possible.

Think about what set you off. What led to the exact moment when you could no longer think straight?

Now identify your physiological state at that time. How did your body feel when you "lost it?" Did your face turn red? Did you cry? Was your breathing short and did your chest feel tight? Were your shoulders hunched forward? Did your head feel heavy? Did you want to scream?

Here's how Mary B. of Louisville, Kentucky, a participant in The Reinvention Workshop, described her memory of "losing it":

"I screamed at my son for spilling his bowl of cereal. When I saw the cereal all over the floor, it hit. My body felt tight. I could feel my blood pressure rising. My face scrunched up. I wanted to punch something. I just couldn't help my reaction."

Please write your three "losing it" moments here:

1. _____
_____
_____

2. _____
_____
_____

3. _____
_____
_____

STEP TWO

- *Identify three moments in your life that you would describe as having unequivocal, life-altering ramifications.*

Such moments may be either positive or negative. The idea is to gain an understanding of the key moments in your life that helped shape you into the person you are today.

Examples of life-altering moments include:

1. *The day your father sat you down and told you he was leaving home.*
2. *The first time you had sex.*
3. *The time when you were in the fifth grade and blew a really loud fart in the middle of silent reading time. Everyone thought you were hilarious from that point on.*

4. *The day you graduated from college.*
5. *The first, and only, time you got into a fist fight.*

Think about how you felt when these moments transpired. If it was a negative moment, were you scared? Did you cry? Did you vow to never again perform the activity that led to that moment?

If it was a positive moment, did your self-esteem fly through the roof? Did you get a huge smile on your face? Did your body feel light, as if you were floating? Did you later try to replicate that feeling as often as possible?

Now try to figure out how you embedded these moments into your psyche. In other words, how did you turn them into character traits that became a permanent part of how you identify yourself and how other people identify you?

Here's how Todd S. of Arlington Heights, Illinois, another Reinvention Workshop participant, described his turning point:

"I remember the exact moment my father told us he was leaving our family. I cried and felt scared and alone. I internalized the moment to mean that if my father, who loved me, could abandon me, then I must have become unlovable. From that point on, no matter how much love anyone gave me, I was always left starving for more. And I would expect to disappoint people and lead them to abandon me, so I would sabotage good relationships before anything bad could happen. I want people to see me as tough so they know to not mess with me or try to take advantage of me."

Please write your three "life-altering" moments here:

1. _____

_____

_____

2. _____

_____

_____

3. _____

_____

_____

STEP THREE

- *Identify how you believe the world sees you versus how you'd ideally like to be seen.*

This is known as a "disconnect" and there's often a huge difference between these two frames of mind. While you may believe your actions reflect your conscious desires, this is seldom the case.

For example, you may want to be loved and appreciated by those within your circle, but your circle may see you as difficult due to your consistent complaining or  obnoxious ways of interacting. Take a moment to give yourself a reality check to determine if the way you want to be perceived by the people around you reflects how they actually see you.

Next, identify your state of mind when there's a clash between how you'd like to be seen and how you're actually seen. When your circle views you as being difficult, do you argue and, consequently, validate their point of view? Do you write people off when they don't "get you?" How do you feel when you act in a certain way to achieve a particular goal and fail?

Here's how James T. from Miami, Florida, an online Workshop participant, described his disconnect:

"I want the world to see that I'm a kind and generous person. However, people seldom care to spend time with me or talk to me on the phone. They accuse me of being self-centered and uncaring. This really hurts, because I know I'm a good person. I go out of my way to help others, yet no one seems to appreciate this. Therefore, I just stop trying. When people do call me after two or three weeks of not hearing from them, I don't respond very nicely. I think I'm trying to punish them for not seeing all of the good I have to offer. I internalize this cycle to mean I must be unlikable, and therefore I act in an unlikable manner."

Please write your three "disconnects" here:

1. _____
_____
_____

2. _____
_____
_____

3. _____
_____
_____

REVIEW OF STEP ONE

In Step One, you were asked to identify three recent times in your life when you absolutely "lost it." The purpose is to help you understand which events throw you off balance, causing you to lose perspective.

Being able to recognize what drives you to the edge of disaster is the first step toward reinventing your life.

Look back at the times you identified. Chances are they happened in response to situations in which you felt out of control.

Identifying similarities among situations that make you feel out of control will enable you to become keenly aware of when you're likely to "lose it." Start to recognize these as danger zones that can create great harm.

It may take you awhile to know what sets you off. Once you do, though, you'll stop reacting in an "automatic" way—that is, the way you've responded until now—and instead behave in a manner that's appropriate to each specific situation.

For example, if you "lose it" when your child spills something, venting may give you temporary relief, but at the terrible cost of damaging your overall goal of a close, loving relationship with your child. As another example, if you "lose it" when someone cuts you off in traffic, your natural response to chase him down and curse him out could result in your getting the tar beaten out of you or even being shot.

Think of your life as a series of scenes that adds up to an epic film. Now think about which characters within your movie play an instrumental role in the outcome of your story. Your movie has lead actors, supporting actors, extras, and so on. Some of these characters have an ongoing presence in your film. Others appear for just a few seconds.

You must become highly focused on the importance of any person with whom you are about to wage war.

If it's someone of great importance to you, look for alternatives to conflict. Conversely, if it's someone of little importance to you, then why bother?

Consider likely outcomes, be selective about which mountains you're willing to die on, and be sure to weigh the punishment against the crime.

GET TO THE ROOT OF THE PROBLEM

Look at your list again and try to identify the cause for your behavior. I want you to become familiar with the circumstances that surround your "losing it" so you can be prepared to control your response when faced with similar situations.

If you can raise your awareness of places where potential trouble lurks, you can begin planning alternate routes of travel.

Try to understand where your difficulties in these particular aspects of your life originated and think about what drives you to the point of wanting to hurt that which, oftentimes, is most dear to you.

Seek to identify your triggers. Examples include:
- Losing your mind when someone is slow to understand you.
- Running away when receiving a compliment.
- Becoming infuriated by a political conversation.
- Or, being in a bad mood for days because you failed to complete a certain task.

John C. from Chicago, a participant in The Reinvention Workshop, used to get terribly upset when he'd have to repeat himself. He eventually came to realize that he associated having to repeat himself with feeling unimportant and "small."

As a child, he was left out of adult conversations because his father often said, "children should be seen and not heard." Ever since—even into adulthood—he unconsciously feared that what he had to say wasn't worth hearing. Anyone not hearing him for the first time triggered that deep-seated insecurity.

Understanding this allowed John to adjust his attitude and take such situations at face value. Now instead of becoming upset when he has to repeat himself, he simply moves closer to the person with whom he's speaking, says the words again, and continues the conversation. End of problem.

Becoming aware of your inner demons will empower you to use rational thought and find the appropriate course of action for uncomfortable situations. When this happens, you'll shift from punishing people innocent of the past "crime" that's upsetting you to experiencing unfiltered reality.

By mastering the skill of seeing situations clearly and reacting appropriately within the context of the situation, you'll join the ranks of a very select group of peers.

REVIEW OF STEP TWO

In Step Two, you were asked to identify three moments in your life you would describe as having unequivocal, life-altering ramifications. The goal is to shed light on the events you most closely associate with your sense of self and to understand how these events affect you.

Look at your list. Some of the moments you've identified may be traumatic, such as a car accident or a divorce. Other life-altering moments may be positive, such as graduating, getting married, or having a child.

Either way, these incidents make up a critical part of who you are.

> ***Your personality, and the way in which you interact with the world, is directly related to how you've internalized your life-altering moments.***

Consider your behavior in relation to the events you've identified. Let's look at a couple of examples that illustrate your power to create the life you desire.

Jackie L. of Indianapolis was physically and emotionally abused as a child. As an adult, she is both untrusting and scared of intimacy.

Though this is an understandable response, others who endured similar abuse have adopted the opposite approach and become warm, loving, and giving people.

Raul R. from Encinitas, California, was convicted of a violent crime when he was 18 years old and served 10 years in prison. After his release, he decided that he never wanted to be locked up again and now devotes his life to helping others avoid similar mistakes.

Far too many people who have been convicted of crimes end up as repeat offenders or walk around full of resentment, blaming the world for their problems.

You have many different paths to choose from after experiencing a life-altering moment. This is the time to ask yourself whether the path you've selected is serving you well.

YOUR LIFE. YOUR CHOICE.

People have argued for centuries over whether we're more influenced by nature or nurture—nature being who you are as a result of your genes and nurture being who you are as a result of your upbringing.

Bottom line: It's irrelevant. You hold complete control over the choices you make now and the wisdom of those choices will determine the quality of your life.

No matter what happened in the past, you can commit to thinking and acting in ways that benefit you from this point on. You can make that decision right now and make it again for every moment that follows.

Recognize that you're not the person you have defined yourself to be, nor are you merely the culmination of your life's events. The character traits you've developed by internalizing your life-altering moments are always within your power to maintain, alter, or fully release.

> *Don't use the past as an excuse for current behavior that serves you poorly. Take responsibility for who you are right now.*

In Chapter 10: Retrain Your Brain, I'll introduce you to methods for approaching life with a blank slate. For now, simply decide that who you are, and how you behave from this moment forward, won't be driven by your past.

REVIEW OF STEP THREE

In Step Three, you were asked to identify three examples of how you believe the world sees you versus how you'd ideally like to be seen. The purpose is to help you understand how dramatically you're affected by the disconnect between these two realities.

Look at your list. If you were brutally honest, what you've written may alert you to lies you've been living. Our intentions are often very different from our actions, and this can create serious problems.

For example, a manager I know considers himself a good boss by checking on the work of his employees several times a day. But his staff considers him a control freak, and most of them are planning to leave as soon as possible for a company where they're treated like responsible adults.

As another example, a father of one of my son's classmates considers himself deeply devoted to his children, but he frequently breaks promises to them when an activity they've planned interferes with his job. Should this pattern continue, over time, his children will lose their trust in him and start to believe that he loves his work more than he loves them.

The disconnect can be buried so deep in the state of Unconscious Incompetence that the person is unable to recognize that a problem even exists, let alone that his behavior is the cause of it.

RECONNECTING THE DISCONNECTS

Disconnected states will inevitably lead to frustration and unhappiness. To identify these states in your life, explore the areas where you experience dissatisfaction and then probe for the causes.

For example, if you're having internal dialogues filled with negativity, or if you're constantly putting out fires, odds are good that a disconnect is at the root of the problem. When you recognize such an instance, think hard about your behavior, the situation or interaction you face, and whether it truly reflects your intentions.

> **To establish a platform of strength and stability, you must be willing to cure that which ails you, even if you don't know what it is.**

If you can move each disconnect out of your state of Unconscious Incompetence and into your state of consciousness, and then make deliberate choices to align your internal dialogue and actions with your intentions, you'll take a powerful step toward improving your life.

"Bonus" Step Four

CAUTION: Take this step only if you can handle constructive criticism from the people closest to you and are willing to risk the consequences.

If you're having difficulty identifying your disconnects, one of the most effective ways to uncover them is to conduct no-holds-barred discussions with those closest to you about how they see you versus how you see yourself.

This step isn't for everyone. It can lead to long-term hurt feelings and can even destroy fulfilling relationships.

With that said, if you have the steely disposition to handle the potential risks, this is the process I recommend you follow:

1.   *Create a list of questions for which you'd like feedback. Here are some examples to consider:*
     a.   I believe I'm a good friend. Do I act that way?
     b.   I feel I'm always there when people need me. How do you feel about that?
     c.   I think I usually have nice things to say about people. Have you found that I actually tend to bad mouth others?

    d. People like spending time with me. Would you say this is accurate?

    e. Based on my history and how I interact with others, I believe I'm a smart person who makes wise decisions. Do you agree?

    f. I feel good about where I work and what I do. How often do I complain to you about my job?

Take the time to put together a thoughtful list of questions so you can make the most of this opportunity.

2. *Start with one person in your closest circle. Do not do this with a group! (You'll feel defensive and attacked working with just one friend or family member, let alone a small mob.) Let this person know you want his honest, constructive feedback. Make it clear that you won't become angry, no matter what is said, and you won't let this conversation affect the relationship. (Obviously, if you can't fully commit to these promises, do not take this on. Simply proceed to the next section.)*

3. *Be prepared to take notes—or, better yet, bring along a digital recorder that's tiny enough to be ignored but powerful enough to preserve hours of conversation. Your loved one has been storing up these comments for years and will have plenty to say.*

4. *Be prepared for a litany of observations that may leave you feeling awful about yourself. Don't get angry or defensive—after all, you asked for this. However, it's ok to request clarification on comments you don't fully understand, and to ask your loved one to expand upon items that really hit home.*

5. *When the session is over, offer heartfelt thanks to the person you chose. Make it clear that you truly appreciate his honesty.*

6. *Internally, disassociate the feedback you received from the person who gave it to you. If the information is accurate, where it came from is unimportant. Simply focus on the discoveries you've made and how you can benefit from them.*

7. *Repeat the process with other members of your closest circle—but always with one person at a time.*

This experience will be brutal. However, nothing will give you more valuable insight into how the world sees you than honest feedback from loved ones.

Once you have the information, use it to repair the disconnects you've discovered. At that point, you'll be able to move your life forward with clarity and focus.

THE VORTEX OF VULNERABILITY: ALIGNING THE PIECES

To complete The Vortex of Vulnerability, examine the items you've identified and look carefully for correlations.

For example, in Step One you might have noted one of the times when you "lost it" as happening in the presence of your father; in Step Two one of your life-altering moments might have occurred when your father abandoned you and your mom; and in Step Three you wrote that you see yourself as a sweet, kind, loving father, but your kids don't call you to say  "hello." This sort of pattern makes it clear that your childhood relationship with your father has had a major impact on your adult behavior.

On the lines that follow, write down all of the commonalities and patterns you notice from reviewing your answers to the three (or four) steps of this exercise. Please take your time on this final step; it's vital to understanding what's buried in Stage One for you and works to your detriment.

Focus on repeated themes, such as "family" or "work," and write down what becomes apparent.

_____

_____

_____

In this final step of review, the negative emotional drivers that lead to much of your unhappiness will float to the surface. While this can be painful, do *not* deny what's in front of you.

To effect meaningful, permanent change, you must be willing to accept things that are hard to bear. If you then combine that understanding with courage and make beneficial choices, you'll have the ability to reinvent who you are.

If the commonalities and patterns aren't evident, don't panic. This exercise is designed to begin creating awareness.

By learning to recognize the moments when you experience discontent, anger, or frustration, you'll begin to identify your self-defeating catalysts. You can then start to take appropriate action.

For now, simply honor yourself for committing to this process of discovery. By doing so, you have embarked on a life-changing journey that will free you from the aspects of your life that have held you hostage without your consent, and worse, without your knowledge.

ON TO GREENER PASTURES

I recognize that The Vortex of Vulnerability can be difficult and may have brought some dirt to the surface. So let's take advantage of that dirt by planting some flowers!

The next exercise, The Vortex of Invincibility, will open your eyes to areas of your life where your soul truly soars. Let the fun begin.

THE VORTEX OF VULNERABILITY— TAKEAWAYS

- Look for areas in your life where you have the propensity to "lose it," feel out-of-control, or experience frustration or unhappiness. These are likely danger zones that significantly impact you.
- Becoming aware of your inner demons will empower you to use rational thought and find the appropriate course of action in uncomfortable situations.
- Being able to identify where potential trouble lurks allows you to plan alternate routes.
- Learn to shift from punishing people innocent of the past "crime" that's upsetting you to experiencing pure reality.
- Your personality, and the way in which you interact with the world, is directly related to how you've internalized your life-altering moments.
- You hold complete control over the choices you make; the wisdom of those choices determines the quality of your life.
- Don't use the past as an excuse for current behavior that serves you poorly.
- Align your intentions with your actions.
- Strive to eliminate disconnects. Seek feedback from others to identify yours if necessary.
- Perception is reality. Give yourself a reality check and be clear on how you're perceived.

CHAPTER 3

THE VORTEX OF INVINCIBILITY

Be who you are and say what you feel, because those who mind don't matter and those who matter don't mind.

—Theodor Seuss Geisel (a.k.a. Dr. Seuss), writer and cartoonist, 1904-1991

Chris Rock once said, "Life ain't short, life is long!" Without being clear on what inspires you and moves you toward becoming your true self, life will not only be long, it will be tedious, boring, and disappointing.

The key to freeing your soul and encouraging it to soar is to recognize areas of your life where you excel.

Once this happens, you'll begin to withhold power from the activities, people, or interactions that dare to clip your wings and concentrate on what brings you the most joy.

The Vortex of Invincibility empowers you to make these discoveries. It is made up of a three-step process (four if you choose to take on the Bonus Step). Each step will reveal important aspects about you and allow you to hone in on your natural strengths.

When combined, the steps will help you identify who you truly are and where you should focus your energy. This exercise continues your exploration of Stage One—Unconscious Incompetence—and begins your journey toward becoming who you were born to be.

Let's get started.

STEP ONE
- *Identify three positive moments in your life when time absolutely stood still.*

At various times in your life, you've experienced this incredible feeling of lightness. It's as if the world melts away and nothing remains but you and your soul.

Some have experienced this feeling when making love. Some feel this profound sense of stillness when meditating. Some feel it when participating in sports. Others tap into it when playing with their children.

When time stands still, you have achieved emotional nirvana. You simply "are" and have zero conscious thought.

Please take a few moments to identify three positive moments when you've achieved this all-too-rare state of peace.

Think about the circumstances involved. Where were you? Who were you with? What activity were you engaged in? Did this happen before or after another specific event?

Now identify your physiological state at that time. How did your body feel when you entered that zone? Did you feel light? Did you smile? Was your breathing full and did you feel completely relaxed? Try to remember as best you can how you felt in the exact moment when time stood still.

Here's how Rick G. of Naperville, Illinois, a Reinvention Workshop participant, described his time-standing-still memory:

"I remember the first time I went sky-diving. All of my friends were nervous wrecks, but I was incredibly excited. My adrenaline was pumping like crazy. I was literally nowhere to be found. My friends said they tried talking to me, but I wouldn't answer. I was completely engulfed in the moment. As I stepped out the door of the plane, I experienced a sense of freedom unlike anything I had ever known. For what seemed like an eternity, the world was mine and I had never been in such an amazing state of peace."

Please write your three time standing still moments here:

1. _____
   _____
   _____

2. _____
   _____
   _____

3. _____
   _____
   _____

STEP TWO

- *Identify the three people you most admire and the character traits they display.*

Over the course of your life, you've encountered an enormous number of people. From friends and family you see often, to TV stars, spiritual leaders or business icons you've never met, thousands have crossed your path.

But only a select few leave an indelible mark. There's no denying that you're naturally drawn to some and repulsed by others.

While many inspire with their accomplishments or generosity, certain people simply "fit" better with who you are. This is not an illusion.

Some say this feeling stems from sharing a kindred spirit. Others suggest that there are astrological forces at play.

The reasons behind this sense of comfort are irrelevant. What matters is heeding the inherent truth of this connection.

Please take a few moments to identify the three people you most admire and the character traits they display. Try to focus on the specific aspects of their personality that rings true.

Think about why each person makes your list. What is it about them that out shines the rest? What draws you toward them?

Is it how they make you feel when you're in their company? Is it what others say about them, or their dedication to honing their craft? Be clear on the rationale behind your choices.

This is how Carol V. of Los Angeles, an online Workshop participant, described one of the people on her list:

"One of my most-admired people is my grandfather. My earliest childhood memories include him and me playing sports, watching TV, or going out to eat. But what I most admired about him was his honesty. You could always count on him to deliver the truth. It was never presented in a way that inflicted pain. He was a master at that. No matter who it was, he was always able to tell them the truth and do so in a way that made them closer. He was one of those rare people who excelled in both his personal and business life. Looking back, I'm confident that his success was due to his incredible ability to communicate effectively. He just made everyone comfortable."

Please list the three people you most admire and their character traits here:

1. _____

_____

_____

2. _____

_____

_____

3. _____

_____

_____

STEP THREE

- *Identify three accomplishments or times when you've been proud of yourself.*

Small victories add up to winning the war. And within these victories hide the secrets to understanding where you're compelled to soar.

By examining moments of excellence, you can extrapolate key indicators that define when you're operating in a manner that's congruent with who you truly are.

From winning awards and completing difficult assignments, to getting the companion of your dreams or hitting the game-winning shot, there were times in your life when you've succeeded brilliantly. Conversely, there were other times when you failed miserably. This is not a coincidence.

Your DNA is programmed to excel in a very specific manner. To fight this is an effort in futility.

As an example, imagine Quentin Tarantino directing Steel Magnolias. It simply would not have been a good fit.

While he certainly could have directed the film, someone would have ended up maimed. It's unlikely this would have meshed with what the producers had in mind.

The same holds true for you. If you're a square peg, trying to jam yourself into a round hole will only result in pain.

Identifying moments of accomplishment or times when you've been proud of yourself will help you develop a clear sense of your personal "sweet spots." These moments reflect circumstances when everything aligns perfectly and you're able to achieve astounding results without expending extraneous energy or overt effort.

These moments may include being recognized for your contributions, rewarded for your abilities, trying something new and completing the task at hand, or feeling amazing because you participated in a particularly gratifying activity, such as helping someone in need.

Try to identify why you were compelled to succeed. Was it because of the person you were working with? Someone you were trying to impress? Or because you were engaged in a skill that came as naturally to you as breathing?

Here's Mark A. from Buffalo Grove, Illinois, a Reinvention Workshop participant, describing a time when he was proud of himself:

"I remember when I was about 15 and my family and I worked in a soup kitchen that our church arranged. We must have worked there for 10 or 12 hours. It was Thanksgiving and there were so many people who came to enjoy a nice, hot meal. I was very tired at the end of the day, but I specifically recall feeling very proud of myself for taking the time to be there and help others. Obviously, we didn't get paid and it absolutely didn't matter. It just felt really good to be there and share the holiday with so many wonderful people."

Please list your three accomplishments or times when you've been proud of yourself here:

1. _____
   _____
   _____

2. _____
   _____
   _____

3. _____
   _____
   _____

REVIEW OF STEP ONE

In Step One, you were asked to identify *three positive moments in your life when time absolutely stood still.* The purpose is to help you understand when you feel most at peace.

Acknowledging these remarkable moments enables you to take a commanding step toward replicating this way of being as often as possible.

By becoming cognizant of what makes you feel invincible, you can begin to direct your energies in these specific directions. It's within these areas of your life that you'll find true fulfillment.

Whereas Step One of The Vortex of Vulnerability asked you to consider when you're likely to "lose it" and plan routes of travel away from such situations, Step One of The Vortex of Invincibility encourages you to steer your life toward the people, interactions, or activities that bring you the most joy.

Robin D. of Los Angeles is a gifted singer. She performs professionally and earns her living on stage.

When she sings, life couldn't be sweeter. The stage is her home and she often works gratis because there's no place she'd rather be.

Where do you feel most comfortable? Even if you didn't get paid a cent, what activities would you enthusiastically pursue?

Look back at the moments you identified and examine what it is about them that you find gratifying. Is it that you're able to engage in the activity without fear or judgment? That you feel appreciated, listened to, or loved? That you achieve a state-of-mind where you can fully focus without interference from outside thoughts? Or is it because you're able to complete what you started?

Embrace whatever the reasons may be. They are integral to what makes you tick.

Try to recognize commonalities in these moments and begin focusing on ways of being that require zero conscious effort, yet create an indisputable sense of comfort.

It may take you awhile to embrace these aspects of who you are. Too often, we concentrate on everything that's wrong instead of everything that's right.

By prioritizing what's most natural for you and pushing what's not to the side, you'll have discovered one of the fundamental keys to living a rewarding life. Now that you have the combination in hand, use it to unlock the mystery of making time stand still.

REVIEW OF STEP TWO

In Step Two, you were asked to identify *three people you most admire and the character traits they display*. The objective is to gain an understanding of who captures your interest and the motivation behind your attraction.

What you admire in others directly reflects what you most desire for yourself. Therefore, it's crucial to maintain complete honesty when exploring why each person made your list.

For instance, if Microsoft founder Bill Gates is one of the people you named, what is it about him that you respect? Is it his business success, vision, willingness to take risks, or notoriety?

If your sister is on your list, what is it about her you appreciate? Is it her openness, ability to communicate well, passion for life, or commitment to love and forgiveness?

Try to pinpoint the characteristics that stand out. By identifying what you admire in others, you open the door to understanding where you're hard-wired to succeed.

Odds are good that you, too, would excel if you focused on these particular areas of your life.

Machiavelli said, "A prudent person should always follow in the footsteps of greatness and imitate those who have been outstanding." The Renaissance politician's wisdom holds true to this day.

Kobe Bryant, All-Star guard of the Los Angeles Lakers, has been compared to Michael Jordan, former guard of the Chicago Bulls, both for how he plays and communicates with the media and fans. Despite his achievements, his replication of Jordan's mannerisms, competitive spirit, and manner of speech is often criticized.

Given that Jordan has been consistently voted as the best basketball player of all time and led the Bulls to six NBA Championships, Kobe should hold no shame for emulating him.

> **While imitation is the sincerest form of flattery, replicating actions and embodying the character traits of those you admire is simply brilliant.**

To further your understanding of this concept, consider those you deplore. What is it about them that makes your skin crawl? Is it their selfishness, cruelty, lack of integrity, or allegiance to something that goes against everything you stand for?

By examining what you loathe in others, you'll find clues to what most aligns with your personal aspirations. Just as two magnets either snap together or resist contact, you naturally gravitate toward those with a similar constitution and are repelled by those with character traits you detest.

Realize the results you desire by acknowledging personal differences, yet obeying the needs of your soul. The map that leads to your destiny is within you—follow it.

CIRCLE OF FOUR

As you embark on your journey of becoming who you were born to be, consider those you choose to travel with. A vital component of your success is establishing a Circle of Four that not only encourages you to reach your full potential, but also accurately reflects who you want to become.

Your Circle of Four is made up of the four people you consider cornerstones. It includes both those you admire—such as a mentor whom you seldom see but have access to—and those dearest to you, such as your best friend or closest family member.

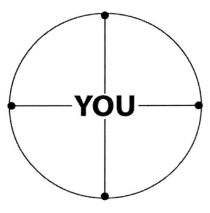

The sum of these four people directly reflects your life. For example, the median net worth of your Circle of Four is likely to be very close to yours. If two in your Circle are broke and two have just enough to scrape by, odds are good you're concerned about where your next meal is coming from.

If your Circle of Four includes three people who consistently complain about their careers and one who is living their *WHAT,* it's likely you want better for yourself but aren't busting your butt to get there.

Be wary of those whose goals and objectives do not closely mirror or exceed yours. While it may be comfortable to surround yourself with familiar faces, it's imperative that they emphatically support your mission or their weight is going to drag you down.

Take a few moments to review your current Circle. Be honest about what you see.

To flourish, you need accountability partners who both inspire and encourage you. Be conscious of the power your Circle holds.

And regardless of whether your Circle has two, three, or even 10 supporters, by aligning yourself with the right people, anything can happen. With the wrong people, nothing will. Choose wisely.

REVIEW OF STEP THREE

In Step Three, you were asked to identify *three accomplishments or times when you've been proud of yourself.* The purpose is to focus on moments when everything clicked and explore why you succeeded.

Since childhood, you've proven over and over that you possess the ability to succeed. Whether it's walking, feeding yourself, or driving, when you've put your mind to it, you've created your desired results.

The triumphs on your list represent natural talents. Accepting these gifts as fundamental pieces of who you are is crucial to realizing long-term satisfaction.

Seek to understand your motivation to excel. Why do you believe you were able to perform in these particular areas?

Were you inspired by a certain teacher? Did you have a coach who brought out the best in you? Did you simply feel compelled to complete the task at hand? Or, were you determined to be recognized?

Try to recall your state of mind. Clearly, there was something that ignited the flame. Take the time to discover what it was.

For example, Jack W. from Lake Geneva, Wisconsin, a personal friend, had been a C student for most of his life. In college, however, he earned A's in every economics class he took.

While he felt he worked just as hard in other classes, he couldn't achieve the same results. Jack recognized his innate attraction to the subject matter and leveraged that gift into becoming an economics professor at a well-respected Midwestern university.

Identifying what compels your soul to climb is critical. The more you concentrate on areas of your life that breed victory, the happier you'll be.

"BONUS" STEP FOUR

If identifying your strengths is difficult, consult those closest to you. Those who care about you will readily support your process of reinvention.

Whereas Step Four of The Vortex of Vulnerability may lead to long-term hurt feelings and even the destruction of fulfilling relationships, Step Four of The Vortex of Invincibility can lead to creating stronger bonds as you enroll others in your transformative process.

This is the process I recommend you follow when asking those who know you best for their opinions:

1. *Create a list of questions. Here are some examples to consider:*
   a. What do you feel are my natural talents?
   b. When have you seen me at my best?
   c. Are there particular people I gravitate toward?
   d. If you had to use one word to describe me in a positive manner, what would it be?
   e. Are there certain activities I excel at?
   f. When do I seem most at peace?
   g. What do others say they like about me?

Take the time to put together a thoughtful list of questions so you can make the most of this opportunity.

2. *Start with one person in your closest circle. Let this person know you want his or her honest feedback.*

3. *Be prepared to take notes—or, better yet, bring along a digital recorder that's tiny enough to be ignored but powerful enough to preserve hours of conversation. Your loved one will have plenty to say.*

4. *Request clarification on comments you don't fully understand. Be sure to ask your loved one to expand upon items that really hit home.*

5. *When the session is over, offer heartfelt thanks. Express your love and make clear you truly appreciate his honesty.*

6. *Focus on the discoveries you've made and how you can benefit from them.*

7. *Repeat the process with other members of your closest circle — but always with one person at a time.*

Each meeting should be light, fun, and inspiring. Remember, you want to focus on the areas of your life where you excel.

Once you have the information, use it to pursue what comes most naturally to you and move your life forward with vigor and dedication.

THE VORTEX OF INVINCIBILITY: ASSEMBLING THE PUZZLE

To complete The Vortex of Invincibility, examine the items you've identified and look carefully for patterns.

For example, in Step One you might have identified one of the moments when time stood still as happening when you play sports; in Step Two, one of the  people you admire is Wayne Gretzky, arguably the best hockey player of all time; and in Step Three, one of the accomplishments you listed was when your high-school sports team won the state championship.

This sort of pattern makes it clear that sports is an area of your life where you feel incredibly comfortable.

On the lines that follow, write down all of the commonalities you notice from reviewing your answers to the three (or four) steps of this exercise. Take your time on this final step as it's vital to understanding what's buried in Stage One for you and works to your benefit.

Focus on repetitive themes, such as "family," "sports," "friendship," or "career" and write down what becomes apparent.

_____

_____

_____

In this final step of review, the positive emotional drivers that lead to most of your fulfillment will float to the surface. Do *not* deny what you uncover.

To effect meaningful, permanent change, you must be willing to accept how you're structured to thrive. If you then couple that understanding with supportive choices, you'll have the ability to reinvent your life.

If the commonalities and patterns aren't evident, don't panic. This exercise is designed to begin creating awareness.

By diligently pursuing where you're most likely to experience peace, elation, and an undeniable sense of stillness, you'll expose your natural talents. This inevitably leads to focusing on activities and interactions where your soul truly soars.

THE COMPLETION OF STAGE ONE

This concludes your exploration of the first stage of learning— Unconscious Incompetence. The following chapter introduces you to the next three stages—Conscious Incompetence, Conscious Competence, and Unconscious Competence.

Get ready for lift off!

THE VORTEX OF INVINCIBILITY— TAKEAWAYS

- The key to freeing your soul and encouraging it to soar requires you to recognize areas of your life where you excel.
- Direct your life toward the people, interactions, or activities that bring you the most joy.
- Hone in on your natural strengths.
- When do you achieve emotional nirvana?
- Heed the inherent truth behind why you're naturally drawn to some people and repulsed by others.
- While imitation is the sincerest form of flattery, replicating actions and embodying the character traits of those you admire is simply brilliant.
- Within your personal victories hide the secrets to understanding where you're compelled to flourish.
- Accepting your gifts as a fundamental piece of who you are is crucial to realizing long-term satisfaction.
- Consider who's in your Circle of Four. The sum of these four people directly reflects your life.
- Strive to recognize strengths. Work with others if necessary.
- The more you concentrate on areas of your life that breed victory, the happier you'll be.

CHAPTER 4

THE NEXT STAGES OF LEARNING

A sensible person will remember that the eyes may be confused in two ways—by a change from light to darkness or from darkness to light; and she will recognize that the same thing happens to the soul.

—Plato, Greek philosopher, teacher and author, 428-347 B.C.

The next stage of the Four Stages of Learning is Conscious Incompetence. As you may recall from Chapter 1, it has the following characteristics:

- You become aware of the existence and relevance of strengths or problems and your deficiency to improve upon or eliminate them.
- You realize that improving your skill in these areas will make you more effective at leveraging strengths or dealing with problems.
- You're able to gauge the extent of your abilities or deficiencies and the level of skill needed to improve upon strengths or eliminate problems.
- You commit to increase skills, solve or eliminate problems and move to Conscious Competence within these areas of your life.

Before entering into the state of Conscious Incompetence, you were living in the dark. Things simply happened, and you didn't know why.

In this second stage of learning, your eyes are wide open and you can make informed choices. More specifically, you're aware of strengths and problems as well as your deficiency in dealing with them.

As a result, you can make a conscious choice to either:

- Take the necessary steps to gain competence in these areas and reap the benefits.

Or,

- Not try to gain the competence, because you don't perceive the potential benefits outweighing the cost in time and energy.

Either way, you can say "I am in control of my life." You're now in a *state of awareness*.

BRINGING TO LIGHT THE CHOICES YOU MAKE

The following exercise will shed light on how this stage of learning affects you.

Please take a few minutes to write about three facets of your life where you possess some knowledge or ability and are comfortable with your level of expertise. Also describe how you feel about owning your incompetence in this area.

Here's an example of what Judy Y. from Ft. Lauderdale, Florida, an online Workshop participant, wrote:

"I know I don't speak German fluently. I speak enough of the language to get by, but my abilities are limited. I'm perfectly okay with this because I don't have any business or social need to use the language."

1. _____
   _____
   _____

2. _____
   _____
   _____

3. _____
   _____
   _____

Now identify three of your relationships that are mediocre in quality, yet you've chosen to maintain them in their current form. Also indicate how you feel about continuing these relationships at this level.

Here are two examples from Jennifer K. of San Jose, California:

"My brother and I haven't spoken for years. Part of me would like to have a relationship with him, but whenever we see each other we fight, so it's really not worth it.

"My friend Louise and I aren't close anymore. It upsets me that neither of us commits the time to get together more frequently. I'd like to talk with her about this and see if we can rekindle our friendship."

1. _____
   _____
   _____

2. _____
   _____
   _____

3. _____
   _____
   _____

This exercise is designed to help you recognize the power you hold to improve upon strengths and eliminate problems that work against you.

The quality of your life depends largely upon your ability to recognize what you can and can't control. Problems falling within your state of Conscious Incompetence are fully yours to own and manage.

STAGE THREE: CONSCIOUS COMPETENCE

The third stage in the Four Stages of Learning is Conscious Competence. It has the following characteristics:

- You have the aptitude to effectively leverage strengths or address problems.
- You can demonstrate strengths and handle problems without assistance.

- You have to concentrate when demonstrating strengths or solving problems as your abilities are not yet second nature.
- You can demonstrate strengths or problem-solving abilities, but you haven't mastered them well enough to do a great job of teaching your process to someone else.

In this stage of learning, you have "concentrated skill." You can achieve your desired results because you have the ability to perform as needed.

Living at this level is not your ultimate goal, though. Demonstrating strengths or solving problems in the state of Conscious Competence too often requires expending a substantial amount of thought and effort, leaving you tired and, in all likelihood, unsatisfied.

To understand why, think about how a professional golfer swings a club. The swing is often compact, seeming to take little effort; and yet the ball scorches past 300 yards. An amateur can swing the club, too, but has to put a lot of thought and effort into it. Further, no matter how much effort is expended, the ball won't travel beyond 240 yards.

To an untrained eye, the two swings may look similar. However, the novice is simultaneously thinking about his grip, set-up, ball placement, take-away, shoulder turn, knees, hips, watching the ball, and more; by the time his club actually connects with the ball, he's already exhausted.

In contrast, a professional's swing is second nature, powered by the unconscious mind. Both demonstrate competence; but the professional's results are markedly superior.

I THINK, THEREFORE I THINK

Please take a few minutes to identify three skills you'd like to elevate from your current state of Conscious Competence to that of Unconscious Competence.

Your skills might include playing a musical instrument beautifully; conducting business; or even being an attentive, sensitive spouse. When you've identified the skills, write them in the space that follows:

1. _____
   _____
   _____

2. _____
   _____
   _____

3. _____
   _____
   _____

Look at your list and consider what it would mean to achieve true mastery of these skills.

For example, think about what's involved in reading this page. Your eyes go over each word, your brain processes what the word means, and you instantly go on to the next word. It happens seamlessly, without conscious effort.

Your eyes know what to do, your brain knows what to do, and ink on paper is immediately transformed into thoughts in your mind. This is the magic of achieving the state of Unconscious Competence.

In contrast, if you're learning a new language, every step of your reading requires conscious thought. First you read the word; then you consider whether you know what it means; then, if you do, you tell your brain to grab the translation for you; finally, you move on to the next word.

When you reach the end of the sentence, you may need to go back and reconstruct what it means overall. You're able to read entire paragraphs this way, and even entire books; but the level of effort required is immense.

Another example comes from my own experience in martial arts. I'm a student of Brazilian Jiu-Jitsu. While I've trained extensively, I must continually use conscious thought to execute most of the moves.

In contrast, my teacher, Carlson Gracie Jr., has attained the state of Unconscious Competence with his

Carlson Gracie Jr. and Carlson Gracie Sr.

Jiu-Jitsu. He has what athletes call "muscle memory." His skills are so ingrained that he vanquishes his opponents with seeming effortlessness and little conscious thought.

When I spar with him, I feel as if I'm trying to fight off an angry lion. I expend a tremendous amount of energy in our sessions. My breathing is heavy. I sweat.

When the match is over, I'm ready for a nap. I feel like I've just been mauled. But Carlson is relaxed and unaffected. Without missing a beat, he proceeds to take on his next opponent.

> *This is your goal—master at least one area of your life so you're able to impose your will without effort, without fear, and with full confidence in your abilities.*

The single most effective way to move from Conscious Competence to Unconscious Competence is practice. So identify one skill that's most important to you and then perform it again and again until it becomes a part of who you are.

Very few people achieve full mastery over any aspect of their lives beyond what their brains and bodies learned to do by the time they were seven years old. Rise above the crowd. Become "automatic" in a meaningful way. You'll be amazed at the power and confidence that results.

STAGE FOUR: UNCONSCIOUS COMPETENCE

The final stage in the Four Stages of Learning is Unconscious Competence. It has the following characteristics:

- Over time, you've improved upon your strengths and abilities to handle problems with such commitment and diligence that it enters the unconscious parts of your brain.
- Your strengths and problem-solving abilities become second nature, enabling you to realize your desired results without conscious effort.

- You can demonstrate strengths or handle problems while engaged in other activities.
- You've mastered the strengths or abilities to handle problems well enough to be able to teach them to others (unless, of course, teaching doesn't happen to be one of the strengths you possess).

When you're at the stage of Unconscious Competence, your strengths and problem-solving abilities have become an integral part of who you are.

Those who master life at this level can appear magical to the rest of the world—because they make something look easy that almost everyone else finds very difficult to do.

I refer to this stage of learning as "the automation zone." Engaging in your top skills or handling problems will be as second nature to you as breathing.

LIFE IN THE ZONE

To understand what life in a state of Unconscious Competence looks like, consider the world's top athletes.

If you're a Chicago Bulls fan, you may remember Michael Jordan in Game 1 of the NBA Finals against the Portland Trailblazers in 1992. Jordan lit up the Blazers for 35 points, and made six three-pointers in the first half of the game.

One of the most unforgettable moments of that evening occurred after Jordan hit his sixth three-point shot. He simply shrugged his shoulders and raised his palms up by his sides as if to say "I can't explain it" as he back-trotted toward half-court.

Playing the game that evening required almost no conscious thought for Jordan. He didn't expend any unnecessary energy contemplating what he would do when the ball came to him.

The process was swift and efficient. He'd get the ball, place himself in position to take the shot, release the ball... and score. It was astoundingly simple.

After the game, Jordan was asked about his record-breaking evening. He referred to his performance as "being in the zone." It was, but that's really another way of saying he was operating from a state of Unconscious Competence.

We're drawn to those who demonstrate "zone-like" abilities. The world's best musicians pack concert halls.

Authors who engage our imaginations sell hundreds of thousands of books. Artists can garner millions of dollars for their paintings.

The world values those who achieve a state of Unconscious Competence. If you follow this path, you may be able to powerfully affect an enormous number of people.

LIVING IN A STATE OF UNCONSCIOUS COMPETENCE

Engaging in events and interactions while operating in a state of Unconscious Competence feels effortless and fulfilling. The periods of achieving this state tend to be rare, but you can increase their frequency by practicing your key skills.

If you focus on achieving Unconscious Competence in even one area of your life, you'll begin the process of living in this magical state more often in other areas as well.

For example, consider the Dalai Lama. He communicates from a natural state of being, without pretense or overt effort. While he's conscious of his interactions with others, his words come straight from his heart.

It's clear that he has eliminated those elements of his life that do not serve him well and achieved mastery over the ones that do.

The point isn't that you should become another Dalai Lama, but that you have the opportunity to redesign your life to meet whatever goals you set.

It all begins with attaining the stage of Unconscious Competence in a single key skill. Once you do so, you'll have taken a critical step toward replicating the "automation zone" for an unlimited number of areas in your life. Plus, you'll find yourself wanting to experience this way of being as often as possible.

THE NEXT STAGES OF LEARNING— TAKEAWAYS

- Conscious Incompetence:
  a. Identifying your strengths and deficiencies enables you to consciously choose the next steps to take.
  b. Weigh the perceived benefit and result against the time and energy required to achieve competency.
  c. You're now in control of your life and have entered into a state of awareness.
- Conscious Competence:
  a. You demonstrate strengths or can effectively deal with problems, but you must think about your process.
  b. Practice, practice, practice until you reach Stage Four — Unconscious Competence.
  c. Challenge yourself to move beyond your given abilities (e.g. walking, breathing).
  d. Become "automatic" in a manner that fully benefits you.
- Unconscious Competence:
  a. Your strengths or problem-solving abilities are ingrained into your subconscious mind.
  b. They are now second-nature enabling you to complete them without conscious effort.
  c. Becoming a master of even one area of your life can result in significant spiritual and psychological benefit for both you and those you affect.
  d. The world applauds and generously compensates those who have become a master of their craft.
  e. You have the ability to inspire the world.

THE FOUR STAGES OF LEARNING: SUMMARY

The Four Stages of Learning is a powerful tool for understanding and reinventing yourself. To truly own your life, you must be clear about who you are and why you do what you do.

Getting past Unconscious Incompetence means opening your eyes to forces from the past that drive you and recognizing strengths that propel you toward your destiny. By leveraging your natural gifts and recognizing issues you've unknowingly battled day after day, you give yourself the ability to redefine your identity and behavior.

Conscious Incompetence and Conscious Competence are all about choosing what to do with the programming that was embedded deep within you but that you're now consciously aware of. They give you the opportunity to hone in on innate talents and solve problems by perfecting pertinent skills.

Once you embark on this path, your goal is to reach the stage of Unconscious Competence. This will allow you to act effortlessly and effectively.

Instead of lacking awareness of strengths or problems, you'll be in touch with yourself and at peace. Ultimately, you'll be able to do certain things so well that your abilities may appear to be magical.

The next step in your process of reinvention is to understand the importance that The Pinnacle plays in maximizing your ability to live life at the peak of your existence. Let's head to the summit!

CHAPTER 5

THE PINNACLE

Man is made or unmade by himself. By the right choice, he ascends. As a being of power, intelligence, and love, and the lord of his own thoughts, he holds the key to every situation.

—Sir James Allen, politician and diplomat, 1855-1942

When you're at your best, fully thriving, and living in a way that's consistent with who you were born to be, you have achieved what I call The Pinnacle.

> ## The Pinnacle is living at the peak of your existence.

DESIGN YOUR IDEAL LIFE

Imagine living without compromise.

Imagine fulfilling your dreams and desires, surrounding yourself with people you love, and engaging in activities that bring you the most joy.

What would you do each day if you could design your life in any way you chose?

Take a few moments to think about this. I want you to dream.

Now dream big. Now dream even bigger.

Assume there are no barriers to what you want. If your optimal life is touring the world, then picture yourself sailing on your 300-foot yacht. If it's playing golf every day, then envision yourself playing 18 holes in the morning and 18 in the afternoon. If it's being married to someone you deeply love, having two wonderful kids, and being the CEO of a well-respected company, then create the image in your mind.

Don't hold back. This is your ideal life. Design it however you like, without fear or limits.

When you're ready to describe what your optimal life looks and feels like, please do so in the space that follows:

_____

_____

_____

_____

_____

_____

_____

Designing your ideal life is a powerful exercise that enables your soul to soar without restrictions. You may find that once you begin the first sentence, your hand can't write fast enough as your subconscious kicks in and demands you recognize what's most important.

This happens because you seldom give yourself the gift of identifying what would bring you meaningful pleasure and happiness.

It's not your fault.

The education you received at school hasn't prepared you adequately for living an outstanding life. While you can read, write, and solve mathematical equations, you were never taught to strive for, and thrive at, the peak of your existence.

But that's ok, because you'll learn to do so now. If you were honest, what you've just written reflects your deepest needs—so heed it.

You have the ability to create the life you want and live at The Pinnacle.

Before you can begin the process of reclaiming your summit, however, it's important to understand how you were knocked down from your perch.

THE DOWNWARD SLIDE

You were born with extraordinary gifts uniquely yours to harness, cultivate, and share with the world.

As a baby and toddler, and even into adolescence, these talents were displayed raw and unrefined.

As you grew older, though, you likely encountered events that caused you to lose sight of some, or even all, of your natural capabilities. These events led you to adjust your identity, moving you away from who you truly are.

Examples of such personality-altering events include:

- Being chastised for acting "inappropriately."
- Being physically punished for displaying aspects of yourself that ran counter to someone else's beliefs or tastes.
- Trying out for something (the football team, the high school play) and getting rejected.
- Asking someone out on a date and being told no.
- Having a room full of students cruelly laugh at you for something you did.
- Being discouraged by friends or family from pursuing your dreams.
- Enduring emotional or physical abuse.

No matter what age you were when the events that affected you happened, you were quick to recognize that behavior X resulted in pain Y. This was all it took for you to bury that particular way of being under piles of emotional baggage.

Physical and emotional anguish subsides over time. The real tragedy is when you never fully reclaim the part of your personality lost during such incidents. An integral part of who you are is banished to the nether regions, never to be seen or heard from again by anyone, including you.

That may sound dramatic, but it's one of the realities of life. You do something that's naturally part of who you are, and if you're slapped down for it, you react. Too often, what gives way is your willingness to expose yourself again to the emotional or physical discomfort you experienced.

> **Each time you relinquish a piece of your core identity, you move farther away from The Pinnacle.**

I call this process of descent The Downward Slide.

Traumatic events aren't the only factor. Another contributor is performing what you perceive as your duty. Whether you had a paper route, shoveled snow, or worked for your family's business, you did what you believed was required of you.

It may be that what began as a way to bring in some extra cash became a straight line to a career path—even if it was work in which you had no genuine interest.

Or it could be that you accumulated so much debt from your schooling that you took whatever job you could find after graduation. It could also be that you turned your life upside down to accommodate your boyfriend, girlfriend, or spouse.

Your good intentions for doing what was right, necessary, or expected of you became the grease on which you began your slide away from pursuing your true talents and passions—and from The Pinnacle.

Once you begin the freefall, it's very difficult to reestablish your footing. Here's a typical scenario:

1. *You go away to attend college.*
2. *Upon your return you want to have your own place because that's what college grads do.*
3. *You take on a job, any job, so that you can afford your own place.*

4. *Bills start to pile up—school loans, utilities, cars, insurance, rent, furniture—not to mention the expenses of actually living life, such as food, hobbies, and dating.*

5. *You finally make a bit of money and you're feeling pretty good, so you buy a nicer car, move to a nicer place, wear better clothes, date higher-maintenance people.*

6. *Now that you have these nicer things, you must continue to work hard to pay for all of them.*

7. *You get married. You have kids.*

8. *You now have more mouths to feed and more responsibility on your shoulders.*

9. *You now have to work harder than ever just to cover your expenses. This might mean working overtime, or taking on a second job.*

10. *The more you look at yourself in the mirror, the less you recognize who you are.*

Chances are the job you started in Step No. 3 had nothing to do with fulfilling your deepest desires or pursuing happiness. It was simply the most convenient route at the time for making money, with the goal of eventually becoming self-supporting and putting yourself in a position to pursue your dreams.

This self-created fantasy is wonderful; but the reality is often more of a nightmare. After submitting to that first soul-deadening job, the downward slide away from The Pinnacle increasingly picks up momentum.

> **While everyone has to pay the bills, too few of us end up in professions even remotely resembling our dream jobs.**

Family and monetary obligations can run deep, and it's certainly possible to feel you had no choice but to do what was required of you or to maintain the lifestyle you created. That said, you must own the fact that from this point forward, you are making a conscious choice to continue living this way.

You can't blame others for the life you've picked. If you're working in a dead-end job, it's because you choose to be there. If you're with someone you know is wrong for you, you're not making the effort to leave and find someone who's right. If you wake up miserable every day because of an event that occurred 30 years ago, you're making a decision to allow what happened in the past control the quality of your life today.

You must begin to fight tooth and nail to reclaim your life and pursue what's most important to you.

The first step may be as simple as giving yourself the time and permission to sit in a quiet place and start trying to identify your Pinnacle.

Some people need to hit rock bottom before realizing they've been on a continuous downward slide. Don't let that happen to you.

Stop your descent right now. You have the power to head back up the Pyramid and toward The Pinnacle. The rest of this chapter will show you how.

Maslow Meets The Pinnacle

In 1943, psychologist Abraham Maslow famously hypothesized a *Hierarchy of Needs* that must be met before your ultimate state of existence—which he called *self-actualization*—can be reached. Maslow visualized the hierarchy as a pyramid like this:

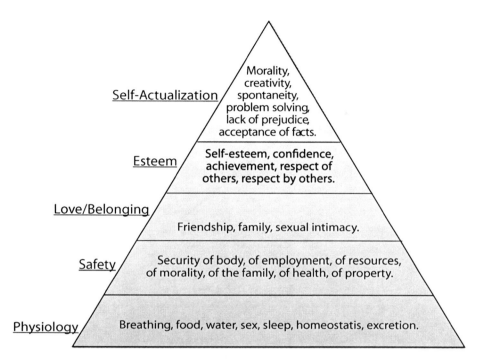

Maslow's Hierarchy of Needs has five distinct levels: physiological, safety, love/belonging, esteem, and self-actualization. And these are genuinely powerful aids for understanding human behavior.

However, Maslow believed that your physiological needs must be satisfied before you can move on to address safety needs; your safety needs must be secured before you can pursue love/belonging needs; and so on. He claimed that it's only when you fulfill the first four levels of needs that you can pursue self-actualization.

I disagree.

From Mother Teresa to Che Guevara, there are numerous examples of self-actualized people who meaningfully affected the world and lived their life at The Pinnacle without having met all five levels of needs defined by Maslow.

I'm therefore suggesting a different way of visualizing human needs, illustrated by the following *Pinnacle Pyramid:*

The Pinnacle

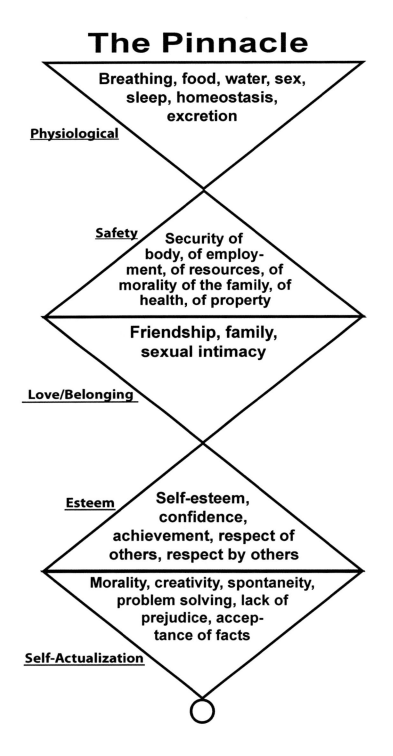

Physiological: Breathing, food, water, sex, sleep, homeostasis, excretion

Safety: Security of body, of employment, of resources, of morality of the family, of health, of property

Love/Belonging: Friendship, family, sexual intimacy

Esteem: Self-esteem, confidence, achievement, respect of others, respect by others

Self-Actualization: Morality, creativity, spontaneity, problem solving, lack of prejudice, acceptance of facts

The major difference between Maslow's Theory and mine is I contend the quality of your life is equally affected by each of the five levels. The Pinnacle serves as the stabilizing element for your life as a whole and enables you to thrive atop the delicate apex upon which your life balances.

To live your life in this optimum state of being, you must become highly focused on the choices you make. Decisions that are incongruent with who you really are can easily send you flying off the summit—and send your Pyramid toppling to the ground.

The key to effective living is to first identify what most directly reflects The Pinnacle for you at each of the five levels of needs and then apply The Pinnacle to your pursuit of those needs.

The following exercise will enable you to construct your own Pinnacle Pyramid. Doing so will help you understand what's most important to you, compare and contrast your current behavior with your answers, and provide a guideline for living that you can refer to and follow.

Let's begin.

LEVEL ONE:

Your physiological needs consist of breathing, food, water, sex, sleep, homeostasis and excretion.

This may seem simple enough. But the choices you make in satisfying these needs spell the difference between living an ordinary life and living at The Pinnacle.

To begin to understand this difference, please think about the following questions and compare your answers with your behavior:

   a. *What types of food are you most comfortable eating?*
   b. *What liquids do you most like to drink?*
   c. *What kinds of exercise do you enjoy?*

d. *Does yoga or other breathing-related exercise fulfill you?*

e. *How many hours of sleep are ideal for you?*

LEVEL TWO:

Your safety needs involve security of body, employment, resources, morality, the family, health, and property.

Being clear on the impact these needs have on you will help you maintain balance. Please consider your responses to the following questions in comparison with your behavior:

a. *Do you feel the need for physical self-confidence? If so, do you practice martial arts or other physical activities that inspire a sense of safety in the event of an emergency? If not, do you instead practice sharpening your mental ability to get you out of dangerous situations?*

b. *Does your job reflect your identity and passions? (There will be more on this later in Part III, Become Who You Were Born to Be.)*

c. *Do your actions reflect your morality? For example, if you consider yourself religious, does your business and social behavior reflect your beliefs? Do you regularly attend a place of worship? If you aren't religious, do you consistently follow your own moral code?*

d. *If your family is of the utmost importance to you, do you demonstrate this by the way you treat your loved ones?*

e. *What do you do to ensure your physical well-being? For example, do you exercise and avoid smoking and stress?*

f. *Do you maintain your home well? Do you beautify it? Do you pay your mortgage or rent on time?*

LEVEL THREE:

Your need for love and belonging consists of friendship, family, and sexual intimacy. Your needs on this level may have been damaged by your past, but Chapter 2's Vortex of Vulnerability should have helped you become aware of these issues and begin the process of getting past them.

With that in mind, please think about the following questions and compare your answers with your behavior:

a. *What's most important to you in a friendship? Do you need a large circle of friends, or do you prefer one or two very close friends? How often do you like to see your friends? How often do you like to talk with them?*

b. *Is your family an integral part of your life? Is your immediate family of overriding importance to you, or is maintaining close relationships with your extended family also important? Do you see your family as often as possible, or do you create space to spend time apart?*

c. *Do you prefer to have intimate sex or casual sex? Do you seek monogamy or prefer having multiple partners? Are you clear on your sexual needs and desires?*

LEVEL FOUR:

Your need for esteem consists of self-esteem, confidence, achievement, respect of others, and respect by others.

Please consider the following questions and compare your behavior with your answers:

a. *From where do you derive your self-esteem? What do you need in order to feel good about yourself?*

b. *How do you maintain a strong degree of confidence? Do you require continuous validation from others, or are you able to establish self-confidence without looking outside of yourself?*

c. *How do you judge your achievements? On how much money you make? On the number of close, loving relationships you have? On helping those in need?*

d. *Are you intimidated by others' success? Are you envious? Or can you acknowledge those who excel and express respect for their abilities? Does working with successful people inspire you or does it make you think about all that's wrong with your world?*

e. *Do you yearn for the respect of everyone? For the respect of a select few? Or just for your own self-respect? Do you judge people by how high they jump when you tell them to? Do you feel less worthy if people don't compliment you on your achievements?*

LEVEL FIVE:

Your need for self-actualization involves morality, creativity, spontaneity, problem solving, lack of prejudice, and acceptance of facts.

Maslow defined self-actualization as "the full realization of one's potential; the desire for self-fulfillment, namely the tendency for the individual to become actualized in what he is potentially." It's at this level, according to Maslow, where you have complete freedom to soar.

Keeping this in mind, please think about the following questions in comparison with your behavior:

a. *What are your guiding principles? Why do you believe you are here?*

b. *How are you most creative? Do you like working with your hands? Do you love music? Does solving complex mathematical equations inspire you? Does coming up with new games to play with your kids make you happy?*

c. *Are you spontaneous? Or do you thrive on planning? Do you like to try new things? Can you adapt to changing circumstances?*

d. *Do you enjoy helping others with their problems? Do you achieve a state of fulfillment from finding a solution to something others could not figure out?*

e. *Do you enjoy taking on all that comes your way without preconceived notions or fear driving your choices? Do you thrive on each of us being unique? At the same time, do you see past differences to a common humanity?*

f. *Are you most at peace when life just is? Do you question everything that crosses your path, or do you take pride in the fact that it has chosen to share its existence with you in that moment? Do you consistently want to persuade others to see your point of view?*

By examining the five levels of needs within the context of The Pinnacle, you can gain valuable insight into what matters most to you. You can then construct a personalized outline for living to focus on those areas.

My completed Pinnacle Pyramid looks like this:

The Pinnacle

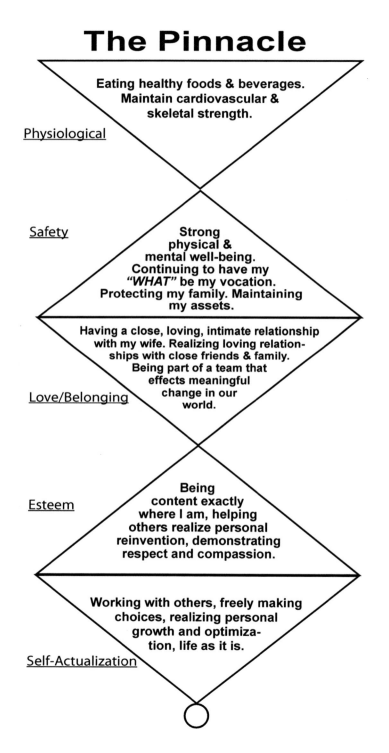

Physiological

Eating healthy foods & beverages.
Maintain cardiovascular &
skeletal strength.

Safety

Strong
physical &
mental well-being.
Continuing to have my
"WHAT" be my vocation.
Protecting my family. Maintaining
my assets.

Having a close, loving, intimate relationship
with my wife. Realizing loving relationships with close friends & family.
Being part of a team that
effects meaningful
change in our
world.

Love/Belonging

Esteem

Being
content exactly
where I am, helping
others realize personal
reinvention, demonstrating
respect and compassion.

Working with others, freely making
choices, realizing personal
growth and optimiza-
tion, life as it is.

Self-Actualization

Think about your answers to the preceding questions and use them to construct your own Pinnacle Pyramid. Keep your statements as concise as possible, yet detailed enough to represent your deepest needs and wants.

Use the following template to complete your personal Pinnacle Pyramid:

The Pinnacle

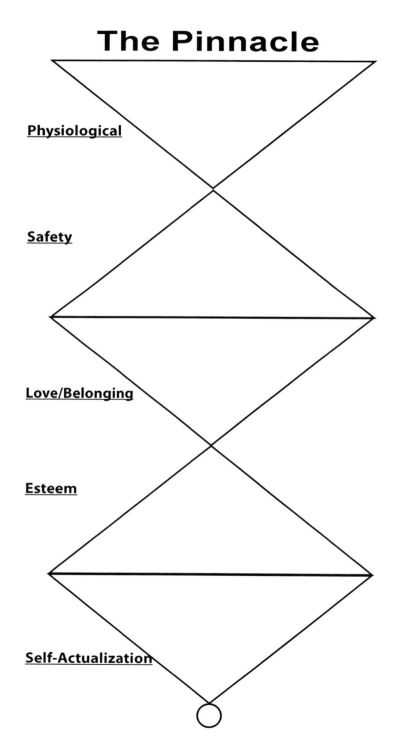

Physiological

Safety

Love/Belonging

Esteem

Self-Actualization

Use your Pinnacle Pyramid as a convenient reference tool to help you achieve and maintain a solid foundation whenever the winds of change threaten to move you off your path.

Attaining The Pinnacle is incredibly challenging. The climb up the mountain is steep, and the terrain is far from smooth.

But achieving The Pinnacle is absolutely possible. In fact, at some point in your life, you were already there. Now that you're aware of how you were knocked down from your peak and understand how to reclaim the summit, nothing should prevent you from taking flight and ascending to your most natural state of being.

THE PINNACLE—TAKEAWAYS

- The Pinnacle is living at the peak of your existence.
- Each time you relinquish a piece of your core identity, you move farther away from attaining The Pinnacle.
- Reaching The Pinnacle is attainable. In fact, at some point in your life, you were already there.
- Being aware of how you were knocked down from your peak will enable you to take flight and ascend to your most natural state of being.
- Stop the downward slide.
- The Pinnacle Pyramid can serve as a reference tool to help maintain a solid foundation when the winds of change threaten to move you off your path.

WORD IS BOND

Completing the process of establishing your foundation requires you to gain a solid understanding of how your word affects who you are.

To powerfully move your life forward, you must fulfill your commitments. Otherwise, nothing you build upon your new foundation will hold firm.

In 1990, rap star LL Cool J introduced the mainstream world to the term *"word is bond"* in his song, *The Boomin' System* ("cause I'm frontin' in my ride and my word is bond").

The term stems from financial markets in which transactions happened so quickly that traders had to work from verbal commitments. It was understood that at the end of the trading day, they'd stand 100 percent by their deals and always uphold their word.

You must conduct yourself the same way—and in *all* areas of your life.

If you commit to being a kind, compassionate, and loving father, be one. If you promise to get X done by Y time, get it done. If you make a mistake, own up to it, and do whatever it takes to fix it.

Your word is who you are. Make your word your bond.

ESTABLISH THE FOUNDATION—IN CLOSING

Congratulations on completing Part I of *JOURNEY TO YOU*. Mastering *The Four Stages of Learning*, entering *The Vortex of Vulnerability*, taking on *The Vortex of Invincibility*, and ascending to *The Pinnacle* are no easy tasks. I commend you for your commitment to completing the most difficult section of this book.

You should now have a substantially better understanding of who you are and why you do what you do. I hope it's clear that the positive choices you make directly support your desired way of being and vice-versa.

You hold the power to choose what to do in every moment and, as you now know, there are only two choices:

Continue the descent, or stop the slide. In which direction will you go?

Before moving on to Part II, where you'll be introduced to *The Seven Life-Altering Principles*, please take a few minutes to review the exercises, your answers, and any material you didn't fully absorb.

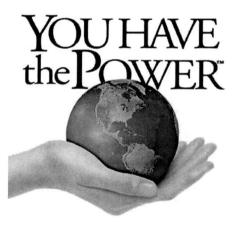

If aspects of Part I were unclear, please take the time to reread these sections. Establishing clear communication in which nothing is left to assumptions is a fundamental aspect of your reinvention process.

After you review the Takeaways for Establish The Foundation and you're ready to proceed to Part II, please do so.

ESTABLISH THE FOUNDATION— TAKEAWAYS

- To live the life you deserve and desire, you must first Establish The Foundation.
- Set anchors deep into your soul. Be clear on your path and don't allow yourself to be blown off course by the whims of others.
- Avoid the "new-car-high" by refusing to succumb to temporary "enlightenment."
- Letting the "old you" come back and overthrow everything you've learned is not an option.
- The Four Stages of Learning is a powerful tool you can leverage to aid your understanding of who you are and why you do what you do.
- You hold the power to choose what to do in every moment.
- What in your life will you master? Or will life continue to master you?
- You can design, create, and manifest your ideal life.
- Achieving The Pinnacle is absolutely possible. In fact, at some point in your life, you were already there.
- Make the conscious choice to continue your descent or stop the slide.
- Your word is who you are. Say it, do it. Write it, live it.

PART II

REALIZE PERMANENT, POSITIVE CHANGE

CHAPTER 6

THE SEVEN LIFE-ALTERING PRINCIPLES (THE S.L.A.P.)

The true key is a trust in self.
For when I trust myself, I fear no one else.
I took control of my life, just as anyone can.
I want everyone to see it's in the palm of your hand.
The past is gone, the future yet unborn.
But right here and now is where it all goes on.

—Beastie Boys, The Update

Whether you realize it or not, you are the common denominator in your life. Even though it may seem like it at times, the world is not out to get you, nor does it revolve around you. However, if you allow yourself to become complacent, you'll end up somewhere you didn't intend to go.

Spending time complaining while you behave in ways that don't serve you well is self-destructive. The key to living with conviction is regaining control of who you are and the choices you make.

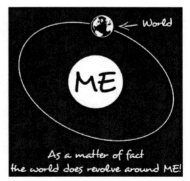

Creating positive change in your life starts with making thoughtful decisions about your actions. Your power to influence yourself will always be enormously greater than your power to influence others.

How different would your life be if you established guidelines for your actions that reflected your true nature? How powerful would you feel knowing that you are clearly directed in your approach to life?

Can you picture yourself with this type of power? Can you envision having this type of confidence? Can you imagine pursuing your life's objectives without fear of self-sabotage?

You can do all this, and more, by learning *The Seven Life-Altering Principles* and making them a part of who you are.

REALIZE PERMANENT, POSITIVE CHANGE

It's a scientific fact that we can undergo harmful genetic transformations—for example, debilitating mutation caused by exposure to toxic substances. But positive, permanent change is also possible.

By harnessing the strength of your mind, you can overpower the genetic limitations of your physical body and the damage caused by emotional and physical trauma.

A study at McGill University found that methylation—that is, genetic mutation brought on by negative stressers such as neglect or abuse—can be reversed by proactive measures, such as a positive environment coupled with psychotherapy. The latter combination has been shown to produce positive chemical changes in the brain.

The Seven Life-Altering Principles are designed to create a similar effect. By embracing these principles, you can reclaim the person you were born to be.

To realize permanent, positive change, I encourage you to adopt the following process. I will remind you of these steps at the end of each of the next seven chapters.

1. Confirm Your Understanding.

After you finish reading about each principle, put the book down and take some time to absorb the concept.

We all have a tendency to seek and conquer. Whether it's learning a new skill, completing a task, or getting from Point A to Point B in any aspect of our lives, we're wired to accomplish as much as possible in as short a time as possible.

This is often efficient. But when it comes to reading this book, the impulse to rush through it works against optimum learning.

To help confirm your understanding, I'll ask you to write down a one-sentence synopsis of the principle. While reading can be powerful, putting pen to paper exponentially increases the likelihood of retaining the information.

2. *Practice the principle.*

After you've moved the concept from the printed page to your written word and conscious thoughts, turn it into actual behavior. This involves:

- Envisioning how the principle can benefit you.
- Recognizing when you're presented with an opportunity to make use of the principle.
- Practicing the principle in real-world situations.

A component of this step will be to jot down a specific incident in which you put the principle into action. Doing so will help further your understanding of the concept.

3. *Live the principle.*

Go beyond practicing and live the principle. Practicing the principle is like trying on an article of clothing.

Living the principle enables you to ingrain the concept into your being through continual repetition. The goal is for each principle to become a part of you.

4. *Share and teach the principle.*

While living the principle, share and teach others about your experiences. Begin with those who can add value to your process of change.

Most animals that travel alone in the wild soon perish. An individual animal's strength, though formidable, is no match when faced with the strength of a multitude of adversaries. We are no different. Your road to reinvention should not be traveled alone.

Sharing and teaching will:

- Require you to translate your internal processing of the principle into spoken words. When you can clearly and succinctly communicate your process, you'll be much closer to making it a part of you.
- Allow you to discuss your experiences and challenges in living the principle with loved ones who will be supportive of your efforts. Answering questions about the principle

will help you redefine and deepen your understanding of the concept.

Choose at least two people you expect will be supportive—family members, friends, spiritual mentors—and share. You'll be amazed at how different the process becomes when you invite others to participate in your personal development. The feedback you receive is likely to be profound and eye-opening. Be willing to be vulnerable.

5. *Make the principle second nature.*

Commit to the process of reinvention by continuing to work the principle. At some point, you'll recognize when you're not consciously practicing the principle and you're simply *doing* it.

Once this happens, permanent change is not far behind and you'll have moved from *Conscious Competence* to *Unconscious Competence* (as described in Chapter 4).

ENTERING UNCHARTED TERRITORY

Reading JOURNEY TO YOU from cover to cover in an uninterrupted fashion should never be your goal. It's not unusual to spend a few days exploring a single principle.

Many of the principles may lead you into unfamiliar, emotionally difficult terrain. If this happens, don't be afraid.

Taking on new emotions, interactions, and activities that lead you into an uncomfortable state of being should be received with an open heart. Being in what you may perceive to be dangerous territory is really your mind and emotions expanding into unexplored lands.

When you feel discomfort, acknowledge it, say "thank you," and proceed on your journey. Remain committed to giving the boot to the limiting boundaries you've unconsciously put into place and move proactively toward becoming a new you.

At times this process will seem tedious. Be patient. You have the ability to travel this road.

Are you familiar with the saying "Wherever you go, there you are"? While it's been quoted by many, it actually dates back to 1440, when Thomas a Kempis wrote, "Wherever you go, you are burdened with yourself. Wherever you go, there you are."

To live the extraordinary life you deserve, you must commit to realizing positive, permanent change. You simply cannot run from who you are.

You can, however, become exactly who you want to be.

The choice is yours... and the world awaits.

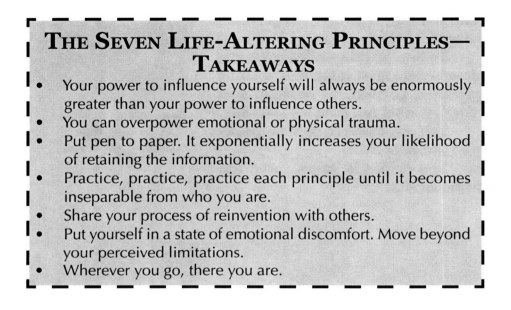

THE SEVEN LIFE-ALTERING PRINCIPLES— TAKEAWAYS

- Your power to influence yourself will always be enormously greater than your power to influence others.
- You can overpower emotional or physical trauma.
- Put pen to paper. It exponentially increases your likelihood of retaining the information.
- Practice, practice, practice each principle until it becomes inseparable from who you are.
- Share your process of reinvention with others.
- Put yourself in a state of emotional discomfort. Move beyond your perceived limitations.
- Wherever you go, there you are.

Chapter 7

Life-Altering Principle No. 1
YāNo

Your life is the sum result of all the choices you make. If you can control the process of choosing, you can take control of all aspects of your life. You can find the freedom that comes from being in charge of yourself.

—Robert F. Bennett, U.S. Senator

Throughout your life, you've experienced hundreds of life-altering events that were completely within your control. They all reflect choices you made—consciously or unconsciously.

The resulting impact on your life is the foundation upon which the concept of *YāNo* (pronounced Yay-No) is built.

There are precise moments, which I refer to as *YāNo moments*, in which you either move toward growing and thriving, or digress in a direction that's inconsistent with your true self.

A key to living a fulfilling and genuine life is taking control of these life-altering moments and choosing the paths that are beneficial for you.

> **YāNo is the principle of recognizing when you're faced with a "moment of truth" that will have meaningful impact on your life, and making the choice that's appropriate and most nourishing for you.**

Please take a few minutes to reflect on your life and think about as many life-altering events as you can. These may include:

- Graduating from college
- Getting married
- Breaking a leg
- The birth of your child
- Starting a new job
- Getting in a fist fight
- Crashing your car
- Making a game-winning shot

Many YāNo moments will be obvious, such as a marriage proposal. However, other moments may seem insignificant if you aren't paying close attention.

For example, you might agree to meet a friend for drinks even though you don't enjoy drinking. Or you might donate money to a politician whom your boss supports but you secretly despise.

The more you agree to participate in activities that don't feel right, the more likely you are to feel your life is out of control. To avoid this, you must address each YāNo moment with equal seriousness.

This may be a hard concept to swallow. How can you pay as much attention to a bar invitation as a marriage proposal?

The answer is this: Any time you undertake an activity without evaluating the impact your choice will have on your life, you run the risk of compromising your state of mind.

Don't get me wrong. I'm not suggesting that you rigidly refuse any action about which you're not 100 percent gung-ho. But I want you to recognize that it's a YāNo moment.

The key to regaining control of your life is to make deliberate choices with an understanding of the consequences. Once you do, you'll stop childishly blaming others for your actions.

If you decide to undertake an activity that makes you uncomfortable, at least you'll have consciously made the choice based upon review of your options. Being resentful of the person who asked you to perform the activity is misguided.

As you practice YāNo, you'll shift to focusing on the potential result of a decision (e.g., the unplanned birth of a child) whenever you're faced with a YāNo moment (e.g., being offered sex without a condom).

As a result, you'll have a greater opportunity to base your actions on what is most true to yourself.

LIVING WITH YĀNO

Living the principle of YāNo is hard work because it requires you to be fully aware of the choices you make. But the more you learn to recognize YāNo moments, the easier it will become.

To most effectively implement the principle of YāNo in your normal routine, do the following:

- Look for YāNo moments throughout your day. This tends to be the hardest part because you're probably in the habit of blowing past YāNo moments without thinking about them. However, learning to recognize such moments will have a profound, positive impact on your life. To reinforce this learning, take a few minutes before you go to bed at night to note the most important YāNo moments you faced during that day.
- When confronted with a YāNo moment, slow down. Take the time to obtain a clear understanding of the situation— including what's expected of you and what's truly right for you.

- Identify each of your options. Recognize that there are often choices beyond yes or no, and consider alternatives to the obvious.
- Evaluate the consequences of each possible path. Try to envision the effect of your decision one hour from now, one month from now, and one year from now.
- Make a choice and then commit to it. After you've put the work into recognizing and evaluating the YāNo moment, step up and own your decision.
- Act on your choice with strength and conviction. If you need to explain yourself, do so with empathy, but also firmness.

At first, this process may be alarmingly uncomfortable. But that's true of almost any journey worth taking.

In addition, this process may initially require you to devote an extraordinary amount of time and energy to it. However, most people get the hang of it within just a couple of days. After that, your challenge will be to reduce the amount of time required for you to work through the process.

Stick with it. As you incorporate the principle of YāNo into your everyday life, it will increasingly become easier; over time, it will become almost effortless.

An Example of a YāNo Moment

Not long ago, I faced a YāNo moment that could have had a significant negative impact on me if I hadn't clearly evaluated the situation and potential consequences. One path would have provided meaningful benefit to a friend and the accomplishment of his objectives, but would have led me down an uncomfortable road. Another path represented an opportunity to participate in my friend's wonderful cause while still being true to myself.

What led to the moment was a discussion regarding "The Prosperity Project," a one-day seminar for high-school and college students designed to teach both financial literacy and the identification of a vocation one can pursue with zeal. I'm proud to be associated with this project and I'm even more proud of my friend for creating it.

When he asked me to be a presenter, I instantly recognized it was a YāNo moment. I quickly weighed my options, decided that participating was in line with my nature and personal objectives, and told him I'd be glad to take part.

My friend is very knowledgeable about economics and finance, and I'm an expert at helping people identify their *WHAT*, so I assumed he would handle the financial literacy aspect of the curriculum and I'd tackle the vocational component.

When we next got together, however, I realized that he'd interpreted our conversation to mean I was accepting responsibility for the entire presentation, both financial and vocational. I'd neglected to base my YāNo decision on a clear understanding of the other person's expectations.

This misunderstanding created a second YāNo moment. To address it, I used the following process:

1. *To avoid another misunderstanding, I asked my friend to articulate his expectations.*

2. *Based on a clear understanding of the situation, I formulated options. I came up with three:*
   a. Tell him "Thanks, but no thanks," and bail on the project.
   b. Agree to present the entire curriculum.
   c. Explain I was uncomfortable presenting the financial material, but would be happy to present the vocational component.

3. *I evaluated these options, considering which one most closely aligned with my true nature and was most likely to produce positive results.*

4. *I chose option c.*

5. *I acted on my decision by informing my friend of my feelings and preferences.*

After a few minutes of discussion, we agreed that he would handle the financial literacy presentation.

This process took little effort. And because I was clear in communicating my decision and the reasons behind it, my friend felt no animosity and we proceeded to jointly create a terrific presentation.

However, had I not recognized the YāNo moment and just gone along with my friend's plans, it would have caused damage. First, the presentation wouldn't have been nearly as effective, since I'm not an expert on finance. And second, I would have resented my friend for putting me in the uncomfortable position of doing his job for him, and failing at it to boot. Both the students and our friendship inevitably would have suffered.

THE YOU OF TODAY AFFECTS THE YOU OF TOMORROW

One of the most significant aspects of effectively managing your YāNo moments is making choices today that will have a positive impact on your future self, the you of tomorrow.

When you think this way, you're less likely to take on payments for something you can't afford; eat greasy foods that make you feel awful afterward; say something in anger to a loved one that might permanently change the relationship; or drive when drunk, which risks ruining or even obliterating your future.

When faced with a YāNo moment, choose whatever option provides the most rewarding long-term benefits and allows the you of tomorrow to look back and give thanks to the you of today.

YOUR YĀNO MOMENT

You're now ready to embark on the path of practicing, living, and eventually mastering the principle of YāNo. To help ensure a smooth journey, please implement the following steps:

> *1. Confirm your understanding by writing a one-sentence synopsis of YāNo.*

_____

_____

_____

_____

> *2. Practice It.*

Begin recognizing when your world intersects with YāNo and practice it in a real-world scenario.

I encourage you to jot down a specific incident in which you put YāNo into action. You can either use the space that follows or your own journal.

_____

_____

_____

_____

> *3. Live, share, and teach YāNo to others.*

Share your experiences with those who will add value to your process of change. Teach what you've learned.

LIFE-ALTERING PRINCIPLE No. 1 YāNo—TAKEAWAYS

- Begin to recognize YāNo moments. They happen every second.
- Choose the option that provides the most rewarding long-term benefits.
- YāNo makes difficult decisions easier as you move from being overly concerned with how you affect others to making choices that are most congruent with your soul.
- The key to regaining control of your life is to make deliberate choices with an understanding of the consequences.
- Shift to focusing on the potential result of a decision whenever you're faced with a YāNo moment.
- Allow the you of tomorrow to look back and give thanks to the you of today.

CHAPTER 8

LIFE-ALTERING PRINCIPLE NO. 2
RECLAIM THE CANYON

Between stimulus and response is our greatest power – the freedom to choose.

—Stephen R. Covey, author of *The Seven Habits of Highly Effective People*

The interactions you face on a daily basis can often be trying. Some guy cuts you off in the middle of the highway. Your boss is on a rampage because the company just lost a big account and your desk is located closest to his office. Your neighbor's dog ruined your prize rose bush.

Many of these events are beyond your control. But what you can control is your response to them.

Most people focus on the times when things are being said or done, but the periods in between are just as critical. It's in these "areas of silence" that you can choose the best path for you. Leveraging this sacred space into a powerful asset will enable you to live the life you desire and Reclaim the Canyon.

> *Reclaim the Canyon is the principle of establishing space between life as it happens and your reaction to those events.*

THE POWER OF THE PAUSE

When faced with adversity—e.g., missing a bus that makes you late for work or having a heated exchange with a friend—how do you normally react?

Do you immediately let the incident take full control of your mind, body, and spirit? Is your day pretty much over from that point forward?

Our reactions are often similar to how we step over a crack in the sidewalk. They happen swiftly, without thought, and with no regard for what we might be stepping into on the other side.

How different would your life be if your first response to an upsetting event was simply a pause—a long, thoughtful pause comparable in size to the Grand Canyon?

It's within this pause that you can quiet your emotions, gather your thoughts and think rationally about the situation and the best way to respond to it.

Of course, a long pause is not always practical. There are times when an immediate response is vital, like when your child is standing in the way of a speeding car. It's for these kinds of emergencies that we're wired to respond in a split second.

For most everyday situations, however, it's perfectly ok to meaningfully pause while you gather your thoughts. Many of the top communicators, such as Nelson Mandela and Ghandi, are renown for taking their time to internally consider many sides of an issue before articulating an opinion.

Knowing how long a pause to take, and how to appropriately vary that pause depending on the complexity and scale of the issue involved, is a skill you'll develop over time. But the first and most important step is to change your reaction from being instantaneous and thoughtless to being the result of meaningful consideration.

COMMUNICATION AS MANIPULATION

Avoid giving others the power to dictate the amount of time it takes you to respond. This is your sacred space.

It's within this space that you have the power to maintain perspective. Without it, it's easy for others to manipulate you.

Both positive and negative communications are, at a basic level, efforts at manipulation. While this may sound cynical, the fact remains that you can't blindly accept anything at face value.

For example, when someone tells you "wow, you're cute," or "you're so smart," or "you did a really good job," the natural response is for every fiber in your being to light up. You instantly assume the person's intent is to make you feel good, and so you feel good about the communication.

However, other people sometimes have their own agenda when they issue a compliment. What if this person needs bus fare and he wants you to be in a positive mood before hitting you up for it? What if the person knows her current love interest is going to be walking by in a few minutes and she wants to engage you in conversation to make herself appear attractive? By not reacting instantly, you avoid allowing yourself to be controlled.

On the other hand, when someone tells you to "go to hell," your first instinct is to believe the person wants you to lose control and become angry; and, in most cases, you do.

But what if this person had a really rough day and you just happened to be in the middle of his hailstorm? What if this person just lost his wallet and is in a state of panic? What if the person is mentally unstable? Maybe the appropriate response is to remain calm and not get involved in someone else's drama, or possibly help the person regain a state of balance.

If you react instantly and obviously, you make it easy for others to manipulate you and you shut out the possibility of a more nuanced and on-target response.

Of course, sometimes things are precisely as they appear. A friend might say something nice to you because she loves you. And a colleague might curse at you because he's truly pissed.

Further, even if a communication is a blatant attempt at controlling your behavior, that doesn't mean you shouldn't go along with it. If the person is a friend or colleague, your interests will typically be aligned with what the person wants you to do. The point is to be aware of what's happening and to make conscious choices.

If you stop to consider before reacting to both positive and negative comments, you'll be in control of how the words of others make you feel about yourself.

Remember, pause first—speak second.

TAKE THE INITIATIVE

One of the key elements of successfully implementing the concept of Reclaim the Canyon is to take the initiative.

Most people believe life simply happens and events are outside of their control. This is dangerously wrong. There are unquestionably times when random things happen, such as a hurricane or an act of terrorism. However, the majority of your experiences are within your control to guide and manage.

To effectively accomplish this objective, establish control of your experiences. This is not as difficult as it may seem.

For example, assume you're driving your car to work. Seemingly out of nowhere, another driver crazily cuts in front of you and slams on the brakes. Your likely response is to become furious, start screaming obscenities, and let the incident ruin the rest of your day. You have totally responded to this experience.

Alternatively, you had the ability to take the initiative as you drove to work. For example, you could have made the effort to be fully aware of your surroundings—checking your mirrors, taking careful notice of other drivers, and trying to anticipate what might intercept your path. In this scenario, you probably would have spotted the reckless driver sooner and slowed down or switched lanes to avoid getting too close to the other car.

As another example, assume the company you own is on the verge of failing, but you have the opportunity to pitch a major client that could keep your firm in the black for the next two years.

You can simply create the pitch based on your experience with previous clients, deliver it, and wait for the client to make his decision.

Alternatively, you can first talk with the client to make 100 percent sure that you understand his needs and desires. You can even make an initial presentation *before* the official pitch to receive feedback and ensure you're on track to seal the deal.

Granted, there may be times when you won't have access to key decision-makers. However, with enough creativity and determination, you can find ways to leave as little to chance as possible, stacking the odds in favor of your success.

> ### *Taking the initiative enables you to gain control of your life by reducing the effect of external forces.*

Leveraging the principle of Reclaim the Canyon will enable you to significantly reduce the apparent "randomness" in your world and empower you to embrace life with open eyes.

By mitigating the effects of the actions of others, you'll avoid being at the mercy of their whims. And consciously maintaining awareness and control over interactions will help you prevent many negative events from ever happening.

YOUR TURN TO RECLAIM THE CANYON

You're now ready to embark on the path of practicing, living, and eventually mastering the principle of Reclaim the Canyon. To help ensure a smooth journey, please implement the following steps:

1. Confirm your understanding by writing a one-sentence synopsis of Reclaim the Canyon.

_____

_____

_____

_____

2. Practice it.

Begin recognizing when your world intersects with Reclaim the Canyon and practice its teachings in a real-world scenario.

I encourage you to jot down a specific incident in which you put Reclaim the Canyon into action.

_____

_____

_____

_____

3. Live, share, and teach Reclaim the Canyon to others.

Share your experiences with those whom you feel will add value to your process of change. Teach what you've learned.

LIFE-ALTERING PRINCIPLE NO. 2
RECLAIM THE CANYON—TAKEAWAYS

- Leverage the area of silence between what's being said and done to choose the best path for you.
- Change your reaction from being instantaneous and thoughtless to being the result of meaningful consideration.
- Avoid giving others the power to dictate the amount of time it takes you to respond.
- Pause first—speak second.
- Avoid being at the mercy of the whims of others by mitigating the effects of their actions.
- Taking the initiative prevents many negative events from happening and increases the chance for realizing positive results.
- Side-step life's continuous drama barrage and handle each moment in an appropriate manner.

CHAPTER 9

LIFE-ALTERING PRINCIPLE NO. 3
THE SUFFICIENCY THEORY

*Do not spoil what you have by desiring what you have not; remember
that what you now have was once among the things you only hoped for.*

—Epicurus, Greek philosopher, 341–270 B.C.

Many in the Western world are on a misguided mission of
searching for the latest, greatest, shiniest, most desired
pieces of crap that money can buy. Others won't rest until they have
the biggest house, fanciest car, and largest bank account.

Then the day comes when they attain what they've been
pursuing. And what happens? Satisfaction and contentment kick
in for a short while and then they begin the quest for the next item
that is sure to provide fulfillment.

We've been programmed to believe that what we have is never
good enough and that we should be constantly striving for more.
There's a destructive cultural correlation between the quality of our
"things" and the quality of our lives.

Yes, it's natural and healthy to want to better yourself. But our
obsession with material possessions stems from Madison Avenue's
advertising wizards, who adroitly lead us to define our sense of self
by what we own.

This may be
good for our economy.
However, this mentality
of dissatisfaction often
carries over to our
personal life.

Continually looking
outside of yourself for
your self-worth keeps
you from getting in touch
with your true needs and

just open your eyes

and see that life is beautiful

eliminates the possibility of generating happiness from within. Striving for external gratification prevents you from maintaining a feeling of contentment that stems from who you are and what you do.

The Sufficiency Theory exalts a way of life based on patience, perseverance, diligence, wisdom, moderation, and reasonableness. In other words, desire less and be less reliant on others.

There is a direct relationship between self-reliance and achieving harmony and balance. By eliminating outside influences, you gain the power to leverage this powerful dynamic and reinvent your life.

> ***The Sufficiency Theory is the principle of attaining satisfaction, peace, and contentment by minimizing material desires and the effect of outside influences.***

THE UTOPIAN MYTH

Many people operate on the belief that when they finally own X, make X amount of money, or have accomplished X as a career goal, they will give themselves permission to take on certain activities that they expect will make them feel amazing. The result of this mindset is that they continually live for tomorrow without ever fully enjoying today.

Think back on your life. Have you ever drawn a line in the sand and said, "When I get to this point, everything I need will be perfectly in place and then I can really start living?"

When you were 18, did you think to yourself, "If I could just get into the right college, my life would be perfect?" After you landed your first job, did you think to yourself, "Sweet! I'll work really hard and after I have X number of dollars in the bank, I'll really be able to enjoy life?"

If so, when you finally reached that magical line, how often have you scratched it out and created another line further down the path? That's how most people in our Western world live.

Our journey typically goes like this:

1. **We set our objectives:** *We arbitrarily draw a line in the sand (e.g., buying a new house, earning X number of dollars per year) and, from that point forward, we're controlled by our efforts to achieve those goals.*

2. **We focus on meeting our objectives:** *We put off things that we want (traveling, having a baby, contentment) until we meet our financial, career, or social goals.*

3. **We believe achieving our objectives is the goal:** *We expect the successful completion of the tasks we've set for ourselves will bring us unlimited satisfaction and launch us toward happiness.*

4. **When we finally achieve our objectives, we set new ones:** *We're happy for a short time. Then we draw a new line in the sand and return to being discontented and living for the future.*

One of the key problems with this process is that we're always looking for external things—riches, fame, awards, validation—to provide internal satisfaction. Happiness is treated as some sort of destination that can be reached by attaining select milestones. And until that happens, we don't even try for pure, unabashed joy ... or attempt to live out our heart's desire.

Beyond having enough to sustain your life, having X number of dollars or X possessions means very little.

However, your internal dialogue associated with these things means a great deal. You can choose to given them power over your life, or choose not to. And you can choose to live within a state of satisfaction and contentment or in a constant state of pause.

Here's the wake-up call: There's no magical place for you to reach at the end of your journey. Nothing incredible will happen when you achieve all your objectives.

> **The utopia at the end of the rainbow—with flowing streams, beautiful people, a pot of gold, and eternal happiness—is a myth.**

To put this in perspective, imagine you want to get married. Each time you go on a date, you hide your true self because you don't want to expose the real you until you've been hitched.

So on a date you're rude, say hurtful things, and are all-around bad company. When questioned about your conduct, you respond: "Don't worry, this isn't the real me. After we get married, I promise I'll be exactly the type of person you're hoping for."

Needless to say, you have few second dates. No one wants to stick around to see who the real you actually is.

Yet this scenario is consistent with typical behavior. We deny ourselves the benefit of the personality we believe we'd display until we reach the arbitrary lines we've created.

If you live your life in anticipation of something miraculous happening, what is this process of postponement costing you? What are you not doing that you otherwise would?

Recognizing that the destination is the road and that the journey is the destination spells the difference between living in a permanent state of wanting and living in a way that creates continuous satisfaction.

Being on the road is itself the victory. You've won.

Don't pine for something in the future. Relax and enjoy the ride. You are exactly where you're supposed to be.

THE SUFFICIENCY PARADIGM SHIFT

In order to truly enjoy your journey, you must reverse the way people typically pursue their objectives.

Here's the process I recommend:

1. **Feel peace and contentment from imagining that you've already achieved your objectives:** *Whatever you've convinced yourself you'll feel once you accomplish certain goals is the way you must start feeling from today on. This shift will powerfully enable you to achieve your objectives from a foundation of happiness.*

For example, if you believe having X number of dollars in the bank will fulfill you, imagine what that would feel like and then create that state of mind for yourself right now. Those who practice the Law of Attraction employ a similar approach.

What would your posture be like? How often would you smile? How deeply would you breathe? How would you treat others? What activities would you pursue? Whatever your answers, adjust your current behavior to match them.

I want you to begin, this very moment, to live out the physiological results of achieving your goals and begin to feel the emotions you've been putting off for the future.

Obviously, you must deal with the constraints of reality. If traveling around the world is one of your objectives and you have $25 to your name, that's not an activity you can pursue right away. However, it costs you nothing to try to feel as if you've already traveled the world and to let that feeling of accomplishment be the foundation on which you operate.

2. **Engage in activities that support the way you want to be:** *Once you start operating with a positive attitude of accomplishment, amazing things happen. The choices you make and the activities you undertake will be markedly different from the way you used to live. And people will pick up on your aura of success, increasing your chances of achieving genuine success.*

Further, you'll free yourself from the pressure of meeting certain objectives before you can feel and act in ways that are most natural for you. In other words, you're giving yourself permission to be who you really are.

3. **Achieve your objectives:** *By feeling and acting like you've already succeeded, you inevitably will succeed... and sooner rather than later.*

This three-step process is the polar opposite of the way we've been trained to achieve our objectives. But it's much more effective.

In fact, many experts suggest you envision the end result you desire to help achieve it. Jim Carrey wrote himself a multimillion dollar check for "Acting Services Rendered" and kept it in his wallet as a reminder of his goals long before he ever got his first big break. He could envision what he wanted and he knew one day he'd be rewarded for his talents at his desired level of compensation.

The Sufficiency Theory is similar in approach. However, when you simply envision an outcome, you're putting off your feelings of fulfillment and contentment until the objective is met. The Sufficiency Theory doesn't stop at asking you to envision your goal; it asks you to live as if you've already achieved it and to use the happiness of doing so as fuel for propelling you on your journey.

AN EXAMPLE OF THE SUFFICIENCY PARADIGM SHIFT

Putting The Sufficiency Theory into practice may be hard to imagine, so here's an example of the process in action.

Desired objective and outcome: Have a baby and then we'll be a happy family!

For a family trained to think conventionally, the process might look something like this:

1. *We set our objectives: We want to have a baby so that we can be a complete and happy family. To accomplish this, we need to have X number of dollars in the bank. Right now, things aren't where we want them to be. We know our life will be complete when we have our baby.*

2. *We focus on meeting our objectives: We work and work until we have X number of dollars in the bank. This might take one year, or it might take five. Until this objective is achieved, we live in a state of discontent because we don't have a baby and how can we be a happy family without a baby?*

3. *We believe achieving our objectives is the goal: Finally, we have X number of dollars in the bank, and we start actively trying to have a baby. One year later, our baby is born. Having a baby turns out to be a lot of work and that little SASK (sleep and sex killer) sure is expensive to have around. The number of dollars in the bank starts diminishing and we feel tired all the time.*

The happiness we thought we'd have when the baby came is not magically appearing. Where is the utopia we imagined for ourselves? Another line in the sand is drawn to replenish our funds so that we can once again have X number of dollars in the bank.

In addition, we draw another line in the sand for when we can return to sleeping through the night. Once these things happen, then we can really start being happy!

Is it clear how the typical process continually breeds discontent? When you're always looking outside of yourself for other people, places, or things to bring you joy, you'll never be happy for long. In order to live a life filled with sufficiency, you must begin to accept and love who you are and what you have.

Now let's look at how the same situation is handled under The Sufficiency Theory:

> **Desired objective and outcome:**
> **Have a baby and then we'll be a happy**
> **family!**

1. **Feel peace and contentment from imagining you've already achieved your objectives:** *Life with my spouse is truly enjoyable. We talk, we share, we play, we love, we fight. Seeing my spouse brings me joy. Spending time with my spouse is one of my favorite things to do in the world. Our family is content. Our life together is meaningful as it is. We've chosen to have a baby, and look forward to our new boy or girl being part of our family. Having a baby will only further enrich what is already a fulfilling life for us.*

2. **Engage in activities that support the way you want to be:** *We don't feel pressure to get pregnant. We don't need a baby in order to have peace and contentment. In this frame of mind, we make love... a lot! One little swimmer hits the target and we're on our way to having our baby. We also recognize that*

Isaiah, Me and Xavier

having a baby will increase our cost of living. One of us takes on a part-time job to help put additional money into our savings account.

3. **Achieve your objectives:** *Nine months later, our baby is born. Since we don't rely on the baby to bring us peace and contentment, our experience in raising our child is markedly different from that of needing to have a child in order to be happy together. We benefit from this state of being. And our child benefits.*

We work together to take on the additional responsibilities of raising a child. It's trying and tiring at times, but our love and happiness help see us through. Our family grows closer as time goes on.

Living the Sufficiency paradigm shift requires a substantial commitment, because we're so used to expecting our peace and contentment to come from outside of ourselves.

I encourage you to start at home with your most important relationship—be it your spouse, your child, a parent, a sibling, or a best friend.

Look at your relationship from a place of peace and contentment. If you want to be happy with your spouse, as Dr. Laura Schlessinger says, "start now by becoming the kind of partner you'd want to come home to."

Give the one you love a massage, cook dinner, encourage your spouse to take a long bubble bath, pick up the dry cleaning, etc. Whatever it is you know the love of your life wants, do it.

The idea is to shift your approach from waiting for certain things to happen to feel a certain way, to feeling and acting in that way now and then enjoying the results you desire. You'll be amazed at how often this results in achieving your desired objective.

Don't get me wrong. This will take a consistent effort on your part.

If you've been rude to your spouse for 20 years, you're going to get a funny look when you offer to rub their feet. Stick with it.

Tell your spouse about the depth of your love, and that you want your relationship to clearly reflect it. You got married for better or worse. Make it for the better. Envision what the relationship should ideally be for the both of you, and then go out and create it.

This process will work effectively in every aspect of your life.

There's a restaurant in Chicago—Ed Debevic's—that's famous for the way its servers interact with the customers. They have fun. They put themselves into their work. Anywhere else in the world they'd just be servers. At this restaurant, they're performers. It's all about perspective.

To be clear, The Sufficiency Theory isn't advocating complacency in any aspect of your life. By no means am I suggesting you sit in a dead-end job or maintain a relationship that isn't working. I am, however, imploring you to implement The Sufficiency Theory before you throw in the towel.

Realigning your perspective doesn't mean denying yourself your objectives. On the contrary, living as if you've already achieved your goals vastly increases your chances of reaching those goals.

You have the power. Your happiness, or your misery, is yours to control. Put The Sufficiency Theory to work and your life will forever benefit. Just remember:

The destination is the road.
The journey is the destination.

YOUR TURN TO ATTAIN SUFFICIENCY

You're now ready to embark on the path of practicing, living, and eventually mastering the principle of The Sufficiency Theory. To help ensure a smooth journey, please implement the following steps:

  1. Confirm your understanding by writing a one-sentence synopsis of The Sufficiency Theory.

_____

_____

_____

_____

  2. Practice it.

Begin recognizing when your world intersects with The Sufficiency Theory and practice its teachings in a real-world scenario.

I encourage you to jot down a specific incident in which you put The Sufficiency Theory into action in the space below.

_____

_____

_____

_____

  3. Live, share, and teach The Sufficiency Theory to others.

Share your experiences with those who will add value to your process of change. Teach what you've learned.

LIFE-ALTERING PRINCIPLE NO. 3
THE SUFFICIENCY THEORY—TAKEAWAYS

- Striving for external gratification prevents you from maintaining a feeling of contentment derived from who you are and what you do.
- Happiness is not a destination that can be reached by attaining select milestones.
- Stop drawing lines in the sand.
- Sufficiency does not translate to complacency, nor does it mean denying yourself your objectives.
- Shift your approach from waiting for certain things to happen in order to feel a certain way, to feeling and acting that way now. The results you desire will inevitably happen.
- No more living on pause.
- The destination is the road. The journey is the destination.
- Remember: You are exactly where you're supposed to be.

CHAPTER 10

LIFE-ALTERING PRINCIPLE NO. 4
RETRAIN YOUR BRAIN

The important thing is not to stop questioning. Curiosity has its own reason for existing. One cannot help but be in awe when he contemplates the mysteries of eternity, of life, of the marvelous structure of reality. It is enough if one tries merely to comprehend a little of this mystery every day. Never lose a holy curiosity.

—Albert Einstein, recipient of the 1921 Nobel Prize in Physics

When we're babies, we have wide eyes, eager to experience the world and learn all we can about it.

At some point, though, most of us effectively decide we've learned all we need to know and shut off that wonder-filled openness to the world. It's as if, as adults, we turn off the record button and proceed to live solely on rewind. The result is experiencing life through a filter of preconceived notions that leave little room for profound new discoveries.

But what if you could return to experiencing things for the very first time? How much would you learn if you felt that everyone you encountered had something to teach you?

You can make this happen. You have the ability to Retrain Your Brain.

Retrain Your Brain is the principle of experiencing life without the filter of preconceived notions.

LIFE AS A BLANK SLATE

Imagine Leonardo da Vinci trying to paint the Mona Lisa over his previous classic, The Last Supper. Or Michael Jackson singing *Thriller* over the track for *Billie Jean*. Or Jamie Oliver preparing his best pasta salad on top of an existing salmon dish.

The result of each of these attempts would be disastrous. The intent of the artist would be lost amid the chaos of conflicting ideas.

How the world would have suffered if our great artists had been unable to spawn new works of art due to their inability to move beyond what they had already created. For artists to realize a new vision, they must begin with a blank slate.

The same goes for you. Your life is being held captive if you deny yourself the ability to create new thoughts and ways of being. When such a repetitive condition exists, growth stops, replaced by a constant state of complacency.

For example, when you want something to eat, you grab a turkey sandwich because you know you like turkey. When you see your spouse after work, you give each other a peck on the cheek and then review each other's day simply because that's your "Honey, I'm home" interaction.

Life is about routine—consistent and predictable. Everything is the way that it's "supposed to be." But you no longer experience the pure joy of being alive.

> ### Try to remember that, at one point, everything *was new.*

My youngest sons, Isaiah and Xavier, live their lives purely from the state of "I want." It doesn't matter what it is. The boys will play with anything they can get their hands on. Xavier will eat nearly anything we put in front of him. When people come over, Isaiah views them as new friends to play with.

For Isaiah and Xavier, life is about trying everything on. Some things fit, others don't. But there's never an internal debate about whether to give something new a whirl.

Throughout childhood and into early adolescence, we're focused on discovery and on personal growth.

For most people, this learning process stops at some point during adolescence. But if we work at it, we can keep our eyes and minds wide open for our entire lives.

When you're able to do so, you have the power to recreate your entire world and smash the rewind button to pieces.

Imagine how different you'd feel if each morning's shower washed away your mental filters and allowed you to take in the day to come as a blank state.

Imagine how wondrous each of these situations would feel if approached as if you were experiencing it for the first time:

- Taking on a work assignment
- Walking in your neighborhood
- Playing with your kids
- Making love to your spouse
- Talking to a stranger
- Watching a favorite television program
- Eating food
- Drinking wine
- Exercising
- Coming home from work

Can you imagine how different speaking with a loved one would be if you put aside the memory of thousands of previous conversations and fully paid attention to how the two of you were interacting? Instead of being rote and repetitive, it would be an exchange of true communication and revelation.

It's important that you break past the "personal language" you've created for yourself. When someone says X to you, you translate it to mean Y. When you encounter an event that's in some ways similar to Z, you simply categorize it as Z—missing nuances that could yield deeper understanding.

The language you've developed is uniquely yours, but if it's all you speak, you'll never learn other people's languages. And if you rely only on what you know to assign meanings, you cut off the opportunity to see the world from different perspectives.

Consider William Shakespeare's famous line from Hamlet:

> **"There is nothing either good or bad, but thinking makes it so."**

For example, you may look at a tree and see life. However, the person next to you might view it as shade. And the person across the street might perceive it as an overgrown weed.

Your life directly reflects the colored glasses you're wearing. Consider trying on a new pair of specs.

Of course, there's much to be said for experience. Learning from your past is one of the points of being human.

This isn't about wiping your memory clean. It's about not letting what you know blind you to learning even more.

The goal is to achieve life as a blank slate as your default way of being.

FREE YOURSELF OF GENERALIZATIONS

A critical step in learning to Retrain Your Brain is to clear away the muddle of generalizations. Lazy phrases such as "that's not me," "that's just how things are," or "people are like that" are too often used as easy excuses to avoid the unfamiliar.

Becoming keenly aware of how often generalizations influence your thinking—and evasion of thinking—is an important step toward achieving positive, permanent change. An integral part of this process is to question your automatic responses.

For instance, if you've never eaten Ethiopian food because you believe "I wouldn't like it," question why. If you don't have a good reason, then the next time you see an Ethiopian restaurant, stop in and pick something up (I highly recommend the Doro Tibs Watt). If you decide it's not your bag, you're out $10, but you gave it a go. Then again, you may discover it's your new favorite meal.

As a more extreme example, some dismiss an entire subset of humanity due to bigotry: "I don't socialize with that type" or "those people are nothing but trouble." This type of prejudice isn't learned from experience, but passed down from generation to generation due to ignorance. Holding onto such generalizations does nothing but cripple your ability to fully experience other people ... and your own life.

> ### Rid yourself of generalizations to open yourself up to options.

In 2008, my family had a birthday party for my son, Xavier, who was turning two, at a terrific place called Pump It Up, a facility filled with huge inflatable play areas and a climbing wall. All the kids had a blast jumping around, going through the mazes, and climbing the wall.

My wife and I had never been on a climbing wall, so we both decided to give it a try. It was a fun diversion, especially reaching the top and rappelling down.

A few minutes later, I looked around and was shocked to see my 66-year-old mother wearing the harness and climbing the wall! It would have been easy for her to say: "I've never done this before, and I'm 66 years old, so forget it." But she didn't let a lazy generalization about giving up on new experiences past a certain age keep her from fully living.

In a few minutes, she was halfway up the wall. She didn't make it all the way to the top (because she had on business attire and dress shoes), but she broke down a lot of barriers with that climb.

Too often, people fail to try something new. Or they may give it a quick try but give up after encountering the first sign of difficulty. Don't be one of those people.

Legend has it that Colonel Sanders had his chicken recipe rejected more than 1,000 times by restaurant owners before he found a partner willing to back him. If he'd simply said, "I guess I'm just not a cook," think of all the jobs that never would have been created and the millions of customers who never would have enjoyed his chicken.

Close the gap between living in a state of wonder and being dissuaded by the generalizations you've unconsciously put in place to limit your thoughts or willingness to take on the unfamiliar.

Ultimately, your life's true power is in the pencil, not the eraser.

COMPRESSION = DEPRESSION

As we get older, we tend to compress the details of experiences into a finite set of categories. And when we encounter a new experience, we slap one of our existing labels onto it—whether or not it's a good match.

While it's convenient to instantly identify anything we come across with something familiar, it can be terribly limiting; it dampens our ability to see things clearly, make exciting discoveries, and grow.

Further, it creates a distorted perspective of the past, which can lead to inappropriate behavior in the present.

For example, if you were constantly praised as a child regardless of what you did, your compression of those encounters might make you believe that you can do no wrong. In all likelihood, this results in having problems accepting responsibility for the times when you screw up.

Further, when someone is legitimately angry with you because of a mistake you made, you don't really hear what's being said because your reaction can't get beyond: "I'm perfect. What's this guy's problem?" This self-assurance may soothe you, but people will grow tired of your being out of touch with the world and stop trying to establish meaningful relationships with you.

Conversely, if you were continually blamed as a child and told you were bad, your compression of those encounters might make you grow up to believe that you can do nothing right. This could result in your feeling awful about yourself no matter how much people like and respect you, react with suspicion when people praise you and, possibly, ruin the chances of reaching your potential.

> ## *Pay attention to how you internalize and compress your life experiences.*

Although this may be painful to hear, a lot of the assumptions you live with every day are built on inaccuracies. As long as you refuse to face reality, you won't be able to distinguish truth from fantasy. So take the time to examine the memories that filter how you experience the world.

Just as importantly, move the processing of your experiences away from compression and categorization. Compression leads to depression. Try to treat each event as its own experience.

THE GIFT OF YOUR PRE-SENT FUTURE

In recent years, virtually every self-help doctrine has strongly championed *living in the moment* to reach your full potential. But that phrase carries a number of different meanings.

In this book, what's meant by *living in the moment* is not allowing past experiences to blind you to what's happening *right now*.

In part, that means paying full attention. But it also means letting go of anything from the past that isn't helpful to you.

If you have a personal video you play over and over in your head, edit that tape to cut out anything that limits you. Or just turn off the video altogether.

> ***Anything from your past that you choose to relive becomes a part of your identity. Be careful about which memories you commit to.***

Every limiting thought hinders the creation of an unfiltered way of being. Think about this the next time you choose to expend energy on something that happened an hour ago, let alone 10 years ago.

It's common for people to catapult instances from their past into their current mindset, so as to continuously relive events they believe shape who they are. But if you refuse to give it power, the past will have no impact on what you do with the brand new moment that stands before you.

As for the future, it represents the great unknown. While we sometimes like to believe that we can predict what will happen, the future has its own special plans and frequently does the opposite of what was expected. Many fear the future, but that makes as little sense as living in the past. You can't control either.

And while living in the moment holds merit, it's difficult to do because life happens by the millisecond. Even with the speed of The Flash, you simply can't capture it.

I propose there's a fourth moment in time over which you do have control, however. Harbhajan Singh Khalsa Yogiji, a.k.a. Yogi Bhajan, former spiritual director of the 3HO Foundation, refers to this point in time as your Pre-Sent Future.

To understand the Pre-Sent Future, picture a treadmill. At the back of the treadmill's belt, behind where you're running, is your past. At the front of the treadmill's belt, ahead of where you're running, is your future. And the spot where you foot lands is your present.

Living within your Pre-Sent Future requires that you continually load the front of the treadmill's belt with exactly what you want. Your feelings, desires, dreams, and objectives—pile them all up in front of you.

Gain a clear understanding of what you want. Establish a plan for living and put it front and center for you to see.

As the belt of the treadmill revolves, the position where your foot lands will be directly in line with the objectives you've defined for yourself. Your next step will be met with

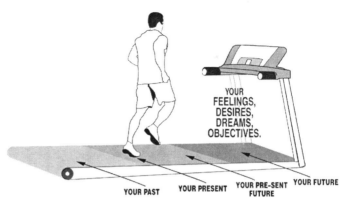

another objective you've laid out in front of you, and so on.

As long as the future is filled with what you desire and create, as the past loops around the deck and makes its way toward you, it will be blocked by all of your future objectives and hold no power.

> ***Put more simply: The Pre-Sent Future is about being in charge of, and creating, the next moment in your life.***

For example, if you covet calm and peace, establish a mindset of calm and peace while anticipating anything that might disrupt it and act accordingly. As Iyanla Vanzant, author and spiritual teacher said, "If you see crazy coming, cross the street."

As another example, if you have a huge project due in a week, split it into manageable pieces and get started now. Don't wait until 24 hours before it's due to begin.

Living within your Pre-Sent Future enables you to eliminate much of life's randomness because it enables you to create the life you most desire by maintaining a sniper-like focus.

If you clearly establish what you want your future to look like, and load your Pre-Sent Future with your desired objectives, you'll operate from a foundation of clarity and strength.

Otherwise, there's only one thing you'll have coming to you—your persistent past.

THE VOICE OF CONJECTURE

A key element of Retrain Your Brain is to understand the Voice of Conjecture and how it rules your life.

According to *Webster's Dictionary*, conjecture is "inference or judgment based on inconclusive or incomplete evidence; a statement, opinion, or conclusion based on guesswork."

This defines how most people live. We're swift to form opinions and seldom allow the time to gather all available evidence before setting our decisions in stone.

Think back on your life. How often have you assumed someone acted out of malice only to discover the person meant no harm at all?

How many times have you sworn off a friend only to have that person end up being one of your closest confidants? How frequently do you make a decision you later regret?

To move toward life as a blank slate, train yourself to gather enough information to make decisions based on facts, not speculation.

The impulse that encourages you to make rapid decisions is what I call the Voice of Conjecture. It leads you to stick with what you know and avoid learning and growing. And the more you give in to it, the less control you have over the quality of your life.

The first step toward freedom is moving the Voice of Conjecture from your unconscious to your conscious mind. This allows you to recognize when it's attempting to impose shortcuts on a rational decision-making process.

Once you become aware of the Voice of Conjecture, tell it to wait while you find out what you need to know to make the best choice. Otherwise, if you keep operating as you always have, you'll realize the same inevitable results.

It's unrealistic to expect the Voice of Conjecture to disappear entirely. It's been a part of you for so long that you may as well acknowledge that it's tenured in its current position.

However, you can work to loosen its hold on you, one notch at a time. The more you do so, the greater the degree of benefits you'll reap from interacting with life as it happens.

YOUR VERY OWN CRYSTAL BALL

Finally, I want you to think about events in your life that you were hesitant, or even refused, to take on because you couldn't know the outcome. Whether it was a confrontation with a friend, riding the new Dive of Death roller coaster, embarking on a new career, or

telling someone "I love you," reflect on as many of these YāNo moments as you can.

Most people will choose what's most familiar over embarking on a journey where the potential rewards are great but the outcome is uncertain. Is that what you did?

You hold in your hands your very own crystal ball—because if fear keeps you from pursuing what's unfamiliar and uncomfortable, it's easy to predict your future.

It'll be exactly like your past.

> ***Your crystal ball shows that you'll be alive in the future.***
> ***But will you be truly living?***

If you're comfortable where you are and don't feel the need for challenges, why consider a different path? After all, you're not hurting anyone, are you?

The honest answer is yes. You're hurting yourself. And you're denying the rest of us the possibility of benefiting from your contributions. You've given up on life and you don't even realize it.

Retrain Your Brain to let go of the past, make new discoveries, and open yourself up to fully experience all the universe has to offer.

You have extraordinary contributions to make and an incredible life to share. But, you must be willing to quiet the Voice of Conjecture and take on what makes you most <u>un</u>comfortable.

Being afraid of the unknown is perfectly normal, but sticking exclusively with what you know is a death sentence. What will your future hold?

YOUR TURN TO RETRAIN YOUR BRAIN

You're now ready to embark on the path of practicing, living, and eventually mastering the principle of Retrain Your Brain. To help ensure a smooth journey, please implement the following steps:

1. Confirm your understanding by writing a one-sentence synopsis of Retrain Your Brain.

_____

_____

_____

_____

2. Practice it.

Begin recognizing when your world intersects with Retrain Your Brain and practice its teachings in a real-world scenario.

I encourage you to jot down a specific incident in which you put Retrain Your Brain into action in the space below.

_____

_____

_____

_____

3. Live, share, and teach Retrain Your Brain to others.

Share your experiences with those who will add value to your process of change. Teach what you've learned.

Life-Altering Principle No. 4
Retrain Your Brain—Takeaways

- Experience life as a blank slate without the filter of preconceived notions.
- Everyone you encounter has something to teach you.
- At one point, everything was new.
- Reawaken childlike discovery within you.
- Move past your own personal language.
- Compression leads to depression. Try to treat each event as its own experience.
- Don't let what you know blind you to learning even more.
- "There is nothing either good or bad, but thinking makes it so." – William Shakespeare
- Anything from your past that you choose to relive becomes a part of your identity. Be careful about which memories you commit to.
- Rid yourself of generalizations and you'll open yourself up to options.
- Take control of your Pre-Sent Future.
- "If you see crazy coming, cross the street." – Iyanla Vanzant
- Keep your past exactly where it belongs.
- Quiet The Voice of Conjecture.
- Embark on journeys where the outcome is uncertain, but the rewards are potentially great.

CHAPTER 11

LIFE-ALTERING PRINCIPLE NO. 5
THE ALTAR OF JACK'S CATHEDRAL

Control your own destiny or someone else will.

—Jack Welch

J ack Welch, the chairman and CEO of General Electric from 1981 to 2001, is renowned for creating a world-class organization through his disciplined approach to management, intuitive decision-making, and ability to bring out the absolute best in his team. His innovative business ideas took GE from a market value of $14 billion in 1981 to $410 billion in 2001, making it the most valuable company in the world.

Many of Welch's concepts for running a successful business can have an equally profound impact when applied to your personal choices. After all, you're the CEO of your life. Just think of it as *You, Inc.* And to achieve success in all aspects of your life, you should run it like a Fortune 500 company.

For example, you must have an operational plan that drives your key decisions, day-to-day interactions, and selection of team members. Without a clear focus on goals, you'll make poor decisions that lead to frustration and unhappiness.

Like a corporation, your life has divisions. You have a personal life, which includes friends and family. You have a business life, which generates your income. You have a leisure life, which includes your hobbies or avocation. And you have a spiritual life, which keeps you centered.

Each part has its own set of operating procedures. A key reason for Jack Welch's success was his ability to keep each corporate division focused on his overall vision for the organization while encouraging autonomy. You should manage your life in a similar way.

You can do so by incorporating many of Welch's best practices into your personal life—that is, stand on The Altar of Jack's Cathedral.

> **The Altar of Jack's Cathedral is the principle of incorporating Jack Welch's successful business practices into your personal behavior. The result is achieving maximum effectiveness in all areas of your life.**

CLEARLY IDENTIFY, AND MAKE KNOWN, YOUR VISION

Jack Welch wore his vision on his sleeve. From day one of taking over GE, Welch articulated an easily understood plan for where he wanted to take the company. Soon there wasn't an employee, stockholder, or corporate partner who wasn't crystal clear about Welch's ideas for moving GE forward.

Though Welch often adjusted his views to fit changing circumstances, he was relentless in sharing his current vision with everyone. This created an exceptionally strong corporate culture.

There was little confusion among GE's nearly 450,000 employees and hundreds of companies around the world as to Welch's overriding philosophy for GE. From the executive level to a brand new hire, choices were made that adhered to Welch's widely disseminated processes for achievement.

The key to business success is to empower those with whom you work to make choices within the parameters of transparent guidelines. Without a well-structured declaration of operational procedures, any choice can be made, and the odds are it will be to the detriment of the company.

Welch worked hard to create a distinct corporate culture for GE and left no room for uncertainty. If a company wanted to do business with GE, it would have to be within a pre-defined set of expectations.

Employees across all business divisions of GE needed to be unified by a defined goal, a single overriding purpose to achieve global success.

And guess what? The same concept applies to you and your life.

The key is to become highly focused on who you are, what your purpose is, and what you stand for. You can do this by establishing a personal Coat of Arms that defines your own internal culture and allows you to be consistent in your approach to all areas of your life.

I'll take you step-by-step through the process of creating your own Coat of Arms in Part IV. For now, simply keep in mind that there's great value in following Welch's example of wearing your vision on your sleeve and for you to behave in ways that exemplify your vision.

Whether you're spending time with friends and family, working, playing games, or praying with others of your faith, who you are and how you interact with others will be unwavering and, most importantly, consistent with your true self.

The Vitality Curve

One of Jack Welch's biggest challenges was maintaining a high degree of team member excellence while developing a system for personnel development that fostered differentiation and potential. With hundreds of thousands of employees, and hundreds of companies spread throughout the world, it was imperative for GE to develop a sustainable system to evaluate the aptitude of its top executives.

GE was too large for Welch and his executive team to be involved with each of its companies on a day-to-day basis. Therefore,

GE's success required hiring, and maintaining, the highest grade of talent available for each company and allowing each unit to operate semi-independently.

To sustain its competitive edge and avoid an unfocused, monolithic culture, Welch and his team created an evaluation matrix called The Vitality Curve. It required the executives within each business unit to rank its managers into a Top 20 percent, Vital 70 percent, or Bottom 10 percent. The underperformers in the Bottom 10 percent generally had to go.

In Welch's book, *Jack: Straight From the Gut*, he wrote: "Making these judgments is not easy, nor always precise. Year after year, differentiation raises the bar and increases the overall caliber of the organization. It's a dynamic process and no one is assured of staying in the top group forever. They have to constantly demonstrate they deserve to be there."

This is an incredibly powerful concept that you can immediately apply. Think about the four key areas of your life:

- Family and friends
- Work
- Hobbies/Avocation
- Spirituality

To help drive home the importance of this concept, I want you to create your own Vitality Curve using the form on the next page:

THE VITALITY CURVE			
	FAMILY & FRIENDS	9 TO 5	HOBBIES / AVOCATION	SPIRITUAL
TOP 20				
VITAL 70				
BOTTOM 10				

To begin, please think about, and write in the top third of the page and the pertinent quadrants, the Top 20 percent of:
- The family members and friends you love most.
- The most fulfilling tasks associated with your job.
- The hobbies that give you the most joy.
- The spiritual endeavors that bring you the most peace and contentment.

It is this 20 percent that brings you 90 percent or more of what you find most fulfilling in life.

Now, take a few moments to think about the next section, then fill in the middle third of the page and the pertinent quadrants, the Vital 70 percent of:
- The family members and friends you moderately enjoy.
- The tasks for your job which are tolerable.
- The hobbies you maintain but don't really thrill you.
- The elements of your spiritual endeavors that aren't entirely satisfying.

This Vital 70 percent represents aspects of your life that aren't sources of great joy, but you can accept as necessary or "good enough."

Finally, take a few moments to think about the last section, then fill in the pertinent quadrants for the Bottom 10 percent of:
- The family members and friends who cause you grief.
- The tasks for your job that you abhor.
- The hobbies you stopped truly enjoying years ago.
- The spiritual endeavors that bring you significant discontent.

This Bottom 10 percent represents the aspects of your life that cause most of your stress and unhappiness.

When you're finished, please review the entire Vitality Curve and double-check that you've included each person, activity, or interaction that should be listed.

This powerful exercise will help you understand what drives you on a daily basis, as well as the impact that various people and activities have on your life.

You're now ready to act on your new understanding:

1. **Establish a plan for addressing the Bottom 10 percent.** As author and speaker Wayne Dyer says in 1992's Real Magic: Creating Miracles in Everyday Life: *"There are no accidents in life. Each experience we have, no matter how painful, eventually leads us to something of higher value."*

The knee-jerk rejection is to want to get rid of the Bottom 10 percent immediately. Before you do so, however, ask yourself what life lessons you're able to realize from these people and activities.

While it may eventually prove necessary to eliminate the aspects of your life that drag you down, first take care to consider why the Bottom 10 percent is part of your world. Understanding what you loathe, and why, can help you better appreciate what you most value and love.

It's also possible that what you loathe hits too close to home. Think about this before making any rash decisions. Keep in mind that when you point one finger out, you've got three pointing right back at you.

That said, if permanently removing these people and activities from your life will vastly improve it, then it's time to do so...with no excuses.

You might protest: "How can I dismiss someone from my life if I have to see him every family holiday?" There are always options.

For example, you can choose to skip attending the family holidays that include this relative and create other occasions to be with the rest of your family. Or you can request that this family member not be invited to events you attend.

Another option is to handle the situation as Jane M., an associate of mine, from Cleveland, Ohio does. Though she loves her family's get-togethers, a verbally abusive relationship with her brother often affects her ability to enjoy them.

Recently, however, she initiated a new plan of action. When her brother says something rude or ignorant—which always happens— she simply takes a deep breath, looks him in the eye, and says "Ok, whatever you say."

This easy-to-implement and empowering approach takes the victory out of his insults by making it clear that she is no longer diminished by them. And Jane is able to continue to take part in an annual event she cherishes.

As another example, maybe there's an activity at work you've become expert at, but loathe with every fiber of your being. If no one else is qualified to take it over, how can you give it up?

One answer is to simply train a colleague to take your place or swap activities. If you play your cards right, you may choose someone who actually enjoys the activity, and you'll have not only lightened your burden, but made a co-worker happy.

Making these decisions is not always easy. But as Jack Welch said, more often than not your life will be the better for making tough choices.

2. **Examine what you've listed under your Vital 70 percent.** *Over the next two to three months, take a hard look at the people and activities falling into this category. Either improve upon your Vital 70 percent so you're able to move some people and activities into the Top 20 percent for your next Vitality Curve, or relegate some people and activities into your Bottom 10 percent and decide how to deal with them.*

3. **Consider your Top 20 percent.** *Quite simply, these people and activities should be the focus of your life.*

Your Top 20 percent accounts for the lion's share of your fulfillment and joy, and deserves the majority of your attention. Think about all of the passion and satisfaction you'll experience from concentrating on your Top 20 percent... and do it.

Leveraging the Vitality Curve will enable you to establish a highly-focused approach to living. I encourage you to create a new Vitality Curve every 6-12 months. Doing so will provide you with clear priorities and help motivate you to cut out whatever drags you down and spend more time with the people and activities truly important to you.

SIX SIGMA®

One of Jack Welch's smartest moves was being among the first to implement a set of practices called Six Sigma. The initiative was created in 1986 by Bill Smith, a senior scientist at Motorola, to improve manufacturing processes and eliminate defects. The concept was so successful that it was extended to other types of business processes, with "defect" being defined as anything that could lead to customer dissatisfaction.

The objective is to eliminate virtually all possibility for customer discontent. A typical business might tolerate achieving a standard of Three Sigma, which is 66,800 DPMO (defective parts per million opportunities), a 93.32 percent efficiency; or Four Sigma, which is 6,210 DPMO, a 99.379 percent efficiency. But a company that achieves Six Sigma standards will tolerate no more than 3.4 DPMO, or 99.9997 percent efficiency.

This may seem like an overbearing commitment to quality. However, a company the size of GE manufactures tens of millions of parts, so even a small defect rate can have significant financial repercussions.

The same idea applies to achieving total customer satisfaction. Even one negative impression made on a customer could result in the loss of millions of dollars of revenue to GE over the lifetime of that failed relationship.

Now think about the four key areas of your life and the effect that maintaining Six Sigma quality would have on each:

- **Family and Friends:** Do you spend enough time with family and friends, or are you away at work on projects that you don't even care about? When you're with your family and friends, are you really there, or do you miss important details because you're distracted by television, your Blackberry, or your thoughts? When you participate in activities with family and friends, do you commit 100 percent to them? Are you fully open and authentic with your loved ones?
- **Work:** When you're at work, do you address your responsibilities with 100 percent commitment? Do you proactively take steps to improve the practices being

used? Do you treat your co-workers with kindness and consideration? Or are you there to simply collect a paycheck?

- **Hobbies:** If you participate in sports, do you pursue each play with total commitment? If you play cards, are you concentrating on what's occurring at the table? If you're an amateur artist, do you put your heart and soul into each piece you create? Are you working toward turning your beloved hobby into a career? Are you leaving no stone unturned in pursuit of perfecting your craft?

- **Spirituality:** When you worship, are you fully committed? Are you actively seeking to connect with a higher power? Are you open to receiving answers to your prayers? Do you always keep an eye out for hints, subtle (and not so subtle) messages, and coincidences? Do you work at helping others? Do you contribute toward helping your place of worship attain its objectives?

Your goal is to achieve Six Sigma in all key aspects of your life. This is highly challenging, but achievable. It requires committing to the people and activities you care most about with your heart and soul, fully participating in all critical areas of your life, and maintaining high standards for everything you pursue.

No one can be perfect all of the time. But you can strive to accept nothing less than your best. Realizing that you're not giving something your all, and adjusting your attitude and behavior to full commitment, is the first step to embedding the Six Sigma concept into who you are.

By focusing your time and energy on the people and activities that most directly support your becoming your true self, you vastly increase your chances of winning at this game called life.

BOUNDARYLESS BEHAVIOR

One last Jack Welch idea I'll share is what he called Boundaryless Behavior. He defined this as "the creation of a boundaryless company where all functions—engineering, manufacturing, marketing, and the rest—would operate within an operational environment that did not have barriers between the units."

Today, this may sound like common practice. But at the time, in late 1989, this was revolutionary. Large, bureaucratic corporations simply did not operate in this manner.

It took several years to implement, but the result of this initiative was the unbridled sharing of information and personnel between the units—and an especially prosperous period for GE.

Applying this approach to your life can reap similar rewards.

> ### How often do you get tied up in Emotional Bureaucracy? Is making a decision a decision-making process in itself?

Many of us get so weighed down in deciding whether to pursue an opportunity that the opportunity either disappears or is taken advantage of by someone else. This ranges from failing to act on a business innovation to letting the girl or boy of your dreams slip away.

For example, when you come up with a novel approach to making something better, or are struck like a bolt of lightning by a revolutionary idea, the universe is giving you a chance to have an extraordinary impact. Have you ever been blessed with such an inspiration and then sat on it?

Like a burning desire that won't be smoldered until it's satisfied, such an opportunity will continue to seek someone ready to fully receive it and bring it to fruition. Remember how you felt when, a few years after your brainstorm, you watched someone else reap the wealth and fame of delivering your idea to the world?

The sinking feeling that you got in the pit of your stomach was your soul kicking you as hard as it could. It's vital to be ready to receive and act upon such opportunities whenever they occur.

The first step is to learn to accurately share information between the various divisions of You, Inc. Let your altruism talk to your greed. Let your happiness have a meeting with your self-destructiveness. Set up a closed-door session for your fear to hammer it out with your hope.

Get the various aspects of who you are freely communicating with each other to eliminate decision bottlenecks. Allow all your top decision-making divisions access to the same data.

You may find it necessary to do some reorganization—for example, firing "reluctance" from his post as chairman of the board and replacing it with "belief."

When you're done, your Emotional Bureaucracy should no longer be a barrier to making decisions, and to your ability to recognize and respond to opportunities swiftly and confidently.

Of course, taking greater risks means you're also likely to make a greater number of errors. That's ok. You'll learn, and grow, much more from making mistakes than from taking no action at all.

> ## When looking back on your life, you'll regret failing to act more than taking action and realizing failure.

A failed attempt at bringing something to fruition does not translate to being a failure. Failure is a word that ignorant people use in an attempt to ground those who dare to soar.

To pass on opportunities is a formula for mediocrity. Commit to internal Boundaryless Behavior, and become comfortable acting quickly and decisively.

MORE WISDOM FROM JACK WELCH

This chapter has covered just a few of the highlights to be found in Jack Welch's *Jack, Straight From The Gut*. I encourage you to read what is one of the most profoundly helpful business books ever written.

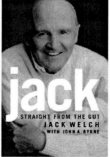

YOUR TURN TO STEP UP TO THE ALTAR

You're now ready to embark on the path of practicing, living and eventually mastering the principle of The Altar of Jack's Cathedral. To help ensure a smooth journey, please implement the following steps:

1. *Confirm your understanding by writing a one-sentence synopsis of The Altar of Jack's Cathedral.*

_____

_____

_____

_____

2. *Practice it.*

Begin recognizing when your world intersects with The Altar of Jack's Cathedral and practice its teachings in a real-world scenario.

I encourage you to jot down a specific incident in which you put The Altar of Jack's Cathedral into action. You can either use the space that follows or your own private journal.

_____

_____

_____

_____

3. *Live, share, and teach The Altar of Jack's Cathedral to others.*

Share your experiences with those who will add value to your process of change. Teach what you've learned.

LIFE-ALTERING PRINCIPLE NO. 5
THE ALTAR OF JACK'S CATHEDRAL— TAKEAWAYS

- Achieve maximum effectiveness in all areas of your life by incorporating Jack Welch's successful business practices into your behavior.
- You're the CEO of your life. Think of it as You, Inc. and operate like a Fortune 500 company.
- Become highly focused on who you are, what you stand for, and what your purpose is.
- Leave no room for uncertainty. Wear your vision on your sleeve.
- Identify the Top 20 percent, Vital 70 percent and Bottom 10 percent for each area of your life.
- Commit to the people and activities you most care about, fully participate in all critical areas of your life, and maintain high standards for everything you pursue.
- Eliminate Emotional Bureaucracy.
- When looking back on your life, you'll regret failing to act more than taking action and realizing failure.

CHAPTER 12

LIFE-ALTERING PRINCIPLE NO. 6: THE NOT-SO-GOLDEN RULE

Love many things, for therein lies the true strength, and whosoever loves much performs much, and can achieve much, and what is done in love is done well.

—Vincent van Gogh, artist

Throughout your life, you've probably been told to live by The Golden Rule: *Do unto others as you would have others do unto you.*

Variations of this notion include: *What goes around comes around* and *as you treat others, so shall you be treated.* Some refer to this circular motion of energy as karma.

The idea is that by releasing positive thoughts and actions into the universe, something positive will come back to you. Conversely, if you emanate negative thoughts and actions, you can expect to encounter something ugly down the road.

The problem with these concepts is that they're built on an unstable foundation of guilt and fear. They're societal constructs designed to keep you from harming others.

While that's a laudable goal, you have to be careful to not be so focused on doing "the right thing" that you harm yourself. Too often we make choices based on guilt or fear of retribution rather than on what's truly right for us.

In this chapter, I propose an alternative way of thinking that will serve you more effectively.

> ### The Not-So-Golden Rule is the principle of eliminating fear or expectation as a motive for your actions.

"MOTIVE DOES MATTER"

"Motive does matter" is one of my favorite quotes from Anthony Robbins. And it's particularly on point here.

Think about The Golden Rule and karma for a moment, and consider what they have in common. To my mind, the most important overlap is that they both promote behavior driven by expectation.

This is self-evident with karma. But even the *Do unto others as you would have others do unto you* message essentially promises that if you're good to people, you can expect them to be good to you in turn. It's an implied social contract.

However, the real world is more complicated than that. Some people read your being nice to them as an invitation to treat you shabbily. And some people insist on your treating them poorly before they'll respect you. Then again, some people have an agenda so unwavering that how you treat them will have no effect whatsoever on their behavior.

There's nothing wrong with the overt messages: Do good. You absolutely should do good. But, you shouldn't do so expecting a quid pro quo. And though you may want to believe your positive actions will pave the road for you with blessings, think again.

Think about the child killed by gang crossfire. Do you honestly believe she deserved her fate because she was a colicky baby?

Or, what about the adult who commits heinous crimes yet is never convicted? Is it possible that, as a boy, he walked hundreds of old ladies across the street and earned his "Get Out of Jail Free" card?

While there are examples of someone receiving a large inheritance after dedicating her life to public service; there are also examples of kind, loving people dying alone after years of living in squalor. Reality consistently demonstrates zero correlation between cause and effect.

Therefore, let the motive for your actions simply be that of wanting to undertake the action. Once you remove expectation, or what the Hindu call Vedas (reaping what you sow) from your rationale behind taking action, only then will you realize the true benefit of serving others.

> *While it's admirable to give more than you expect to receive, giving more than you believe you're able to give manifests long-term contentment.*

Begin questioning your motives. What is it that you expect to receive in return for your efforts?

The point of The Not-So-Golden Rule is to eliminate all ties to expectation. This will allow your motive for action to shift from anticipating a certain response to acting simply because you choose to.

Once you can get to the point of expecting nothing in return for your actions, you will be in a position to receive everything.

LET LOVE RULE

For the past several years, I've been tuning in to Dr. Laura Schlessinger. At first, I found her brash, often insensitive, and sometimes just mean.

After listening to her for a while, however, I began to understand that while her on-air approach takes a no-nonsense, no-holds-barred stance with callers, her method of counseling is built on a foundation of love.

Schlessinger has an uncanny ability to know when a caller needs a swift kick in the rear. Her tough-love tactics are never meant to deliver pain, but to free callers from whatever emotional muck they're stuck in and move them onward and upward.

Dr. Laura has clearly identified her framework for living. Her counseling is consistent. Her style is unwavering.

Though some who call in don't get the answers they were hoping to hear, her advice is always consistent with her principles. Countless times over the years, I've heard someone who fought Dr. Laura tooth and nail over her advice call back a few weeks later to say that the suggestions really worked.

What amazes me most about Dr. Laura is how much she really does care about each and every caller. There are those she can't help because they just don't want to be helped but, the vast majority of the time, a caller leaves with a new perspective and a new positive attitude.

It's because of her commitment to love, without the expectation of reciprocation, that Dr. Laura has built one of the biggest brands in all of radio.

> *One of Dr. Laura's overriding principles is being the person you want to come home to. If you're married, pamper your spouse. Say sweet nothings. Bring breakfast to bed. Make your home an oasis.*

That may sound similar to *The Golden Rule* or karma. The key difference, however, is to act out of love, without the expectation of *anything* in return.

You love because you want to, not because you need that person to love you back. Of course, the latter might happen.

But there's a big difference between saying "I love you" because you want to be loved, and saying it simply because you want to express how you feel.

It's possible to find love in everything you do. Whether at work, with family and friends, in your hobbies or avocation, or at your place of worship, look for love and act on it. Period.

In the words of my favorite musician, Lenny Kravitz: *"Let Love Rule."* It's within this pure state of effortless bliss that you'll find peace and contentment.

By establishing love as the ruler of your domain, and taking action without expectation of reward, you'll realize spiritual wealth of far greater value than gold.

YOUR TURN TO CREATE YOUR OWN RULES

You're now ready to embark on the path of practicing, living, and eventually mastering the principle of The Not-So-Golden Rule. To help ensure a smooth journey, please implement the following steps:

1. *Confirm your understanding by writing a one-sentence synopsis of The Not-So-Golden Rule.*

_____

_____

_____

_____

2. *Practice it.*

Begin recognizing when your world intersects with The Not-So-Golden Rule and practice its teachings in a real-world scenario.

I encourage you to jot down a specific incident in which you put The Not-So-Golden Rule into action. You can either use the space that follows or your own private journal.

_____

_____

_____

_____

3. *Live, share and teach The Not-So-Golden Rule to others.*

Share your experiences with those who will add value to your process of change. Teach what you've learned.

LIFE-ALTERING PRINCIPLE NO. 6
THE NOT-SO-GOLDEN RULE—
TAKEAWAYS

- Expect nothing from your actions. Put yourself in position to receive everything.
- Eliminate the perceived correlation between your actions and the results realized.
- Establish love as the ruler of your domain.
- Motive does matter. Question yours.
- Find love in everything you do.
- In a state of pure, effortless bliss is where you'll find peace and contentment.
- Give much more than you believe you are able to give.

CHAPTER 13

LIFE-ALTERING PRINCIPLE No. 7
THE SLOW DEATH OF NOT
BEING THE STAR

The critic has to educate the public; the artist has to educate the critic.
—Oscar Wilde, writer, poet and playwright, 1854-1900

Tens of millions of people know who the celebrity of the moment is dating.

But only a fraction of that vast audience can plainly state what they want for themselves.

And an even smaller number have a six-month or one-year plan for reaching their goals.

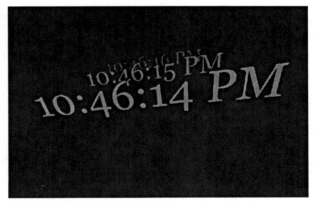

Why are so many driven to live vicariously through others? Why do some spend hours in the rain just to catch a glimpse of a popular actor? Why do some feel more connected to a top-selling musician than to people they see every day?

The answer to all of these questions is the same: We're naturally attracted to those who are living their lives to the fullest, people who have connected to their true selves.

It's time to recognize that you, too, hold this potential. You have the power to become exactly the type of person you aspire to be.

When you squander your time pursuing activities that provide no direct benefit, you slide further away from The Pinnacle (described in Chapter 5). As a result, you operate from a place of discontent which makes you feel even more of a need to attach yourself to those you admire.

Such distractions will provide only momentary relief, though. Until you become who you were born to be, your soul will make it clear that you have yet to realize your full potential.

You can be the star. Shake off the slumber and awaken to the fact that all roads in the state of distraction lead to *The Slow Death of Not Being the Star.*

> **The Slow Death of Not Being the Star is the principle of shifting focus away from time-consuming distractions and toward the pursuit of your personal goals.**

TAKE INVENTORY OF YOUR CURRENT DISTRACTIONS

According to Nielsen, the average American watches more than 151 hours of television per month. Considering we sleep around eight hours a day, that means most of us spend more than 31 percent of our waking hours in front of a TV.

But that's not the end of it. There's going to movies, attending sports events, listening to music, surfing the Net...for most of us, such non-work related activities add up to more than 50 percent of our waking life!

If immersing yourself in pop culture or the arts is your way of pursuing your true self, then the rest of this chapter might not apply to you. If not, you may be frittering away too much of your precious time on being entertained by others.

An easy way to find out is to buy a small notebook. For one week, write down how you spend the hours of each day.

Specifically, write down the time that each activity begins and ends. Or simply mark the number of minutes you devote to each activity.

At the end of the week, pull out your notebook and tally up how much time you devoted to pursuing your life's goals and how much time you spent being distracted.

The results may shock you. Chances are you'll find that what you've been thinking of as relaxing "downtime" is actually the dominant force in your life, devouring enormous amounts of time you can never get back.

THE TWO WAYS TO USE YOUR TIME

Though we all like to think of ourselves as immortal, the truth is that our time on Earth is finite—and precious. So it's important to use it wisely.

I believe there are only two ways to use your time: *Spend* it or *Invest* it.

Spending Your Time

Spending your time is essentially the same as spending money.

You have a limited amount of money, and you spend it to fill various needs and desires. Once you use up the money, it's no longer available for buying something else.

The same is true of your time. When you choose to devote an hour to something that doesn't advance your life's goals, you've spent that time.

It's no longer yours to use; and there's nothing you can do to get it back. You weighed your options as to what you could do with your time, and you chose to spend it on an activity that didn't help you become who you want to be.

Investing Your Time

Investing money typically means putting your assets into stocks, real estate, and other areas that—you hope—will pay off in the long term.

Similarly, investing time means focusing on activities that—you hope—will reap meaningful rewards, both as you're doing them and down the road.

Quite simply, this is focusing your time on realizing your hopes and dreams.

CREATION FROM SCRATCH

Instead of spending most of your time consuming the creations of others, consider focusing your time on becoming a creator.

Creators are a rare breed. Only a small number of people have the patience, will, and guts necessary to take something from an idea to a tangible form and put it out there for the world to judge.

Virtually everyone is a critic.

> ### It's easy to be a critic,
> ### but hard to be a creator.

Think about it. You go see a movie, watch a TV show, or read a book and you immediately have an opinion.

When was the last time you put something forward to be critiqued? Better yet, when was the last time you created something you weren't asked to create?

When you were a child, you created things all the time. You drew, you painted, you made statues out of Play-Doh, and you made up stories for you and your friends to take part in.

If you're an artist or inventor, then you never really gave up these activities. Otherwise, you probably did. At some identifiable point, your period of creation came to a screeching halt.

It could have happened for any number of reasons. Maybe when you were 5, someone said your game was dumb, and from that point forward you wouldn't put yourself out on a limb again. Or maybe when you were 7 your parents told you to stop getting paint on the floor and you decided that art wasn't worth the risk of being yelled at.

Now ask yourself this question: "How long am I going to let these moments in my past control who I am today?"

Your answer must be: *"Not one second longer!"*

Stop continuing to give power to those who have long since moved beyond whatever it was that happened years ago. That includes you.

> ### *Don't let your past control you. Whatever the reasons were that drove you to stifle your creative process—let them go.*

The time for you to rekindle your creative energy is *now*.

There's only one you. You're unlike anyone else on this planet and you have unique gifts to share and important contributions to make.

If you have the talent, the passion, and the dedication to leverage those gifts, you can become a creator. And maybe one day... a star.

DEFINING WHAT IT MEANS TO BE THE STAR

In this book, being a *star* doesn't necessarily mean getting the lead role in a movie or selling out a rock concert. Only a select few have the talent and desire to do that.

What I mean by *star* is connecting to your true self and living your life to the fullest.

For one person, that might mean becoming an amazingly inspirational second-grade teacher. For another, it might mean being an exceptionally gentle and popular dentist.

As long as you're being true to yourself, it doesn't matter what career you choose to become a star. Nor is it important whether the stage you choose is for a relatively small audience or for millions.

What counts most is that you pursue what's right for you and that you consistently give 100 percent of yourself to achieve the best performance.

If you're great at what you do, recognition will follow. And while being recognized as a *star* may not be your goal, your example will inspire others to follow their life's path—which should be worth any temporary discomfort you experience from your celebrity.

GET A BIGGER PLATE

One of the most common excuses I hear for not pursuing stardom is: "I don't have time. My plate is full."

However, as explained earlier in this chapter, you'll typically have opportunities over the course of any day to devote a meaningful amount of time to achieving your life's goals. It's a matter of prioritizing so that you minimize spending time and focus on investing it.

This book was written over the course of 26 months. With two young boys at home, (ages 2 and 5 when I started writing), three active business units (The Reinvention Workshop, Bold Development and Liquor.com), a wife, a social life, Jiu-Jitsu, golf, and other endeavors, finding time to complete this book was not always easy.

As I write this paragraph, my boys are screaming in the background as one of their robot destroyer toys makes its way down the hall singing its battle cry. I often work at home, so writing in silence is rare.

I created this book by snatching stray hours during the day, making a habit of writing immediately after putting the kids to bed, and setting aside more than a few Saturdays and Sundays. Because completing this book was a priority, I used every available moment I could find to get it done.

> ## *Avoid the time sucks. Your life is at stake.*

You'll be amazed at how much you can get done if you put your mind to it. If necessary, schedule your day so you have a clear understanding of what you'll be doing and for how long.

Take control of your time... and then take on more than you believe you can handle.

Get rid of the kid-size Elmo saucer that you've been balancing your life on. You're ready for a bigger plate.

HOW DO I BEGIN THE PROCESS OF BEING THE STAR?

It's easy to become enchanted with the lives of others. It's fine to be inspired by their accomplishments and to learn from their examples.

But when you spend your days obsessing about those you believe are "living the dream," you lose precious time you could be investing in the creation of your own ideal life. Instead, decide to become a star, then focus your time and energy on making it happen.

Making this choice is the first vital step in your ascension to stardom. The third part of this book, "Become Who You Were Born to Be" will guide you through the next steps, which focus on identifying what you were born to do.

YOUR TURN TO BE THE STAR

You're now ready to embark on the path of practicing, living, and eventually mastering the principle of The Slow Death of Not Being the Star. To help ensure a smooth journey, please implement the following steps:

1. *Confirm your understanding by writing a one-sentence synopsis of The Slow Death of Not Being the Star.*

   _____

   _____

   _____

   _____

2. *Practice it.*

   Begin recognizing when your world intersects with The Slow Death of Not Being the Star and practice its teachings in a real-world scenario.

   I encourage you to jot down a specific incident in which you put The Slow Death of Not Being the Star into action. You can either use the space below or your own private journal.

   _____

   _____

   _____

   _____

3. *Live, share, and teach The Slow Death of Not Being the Star to others.*

   Share your experiences with those who will add value to your process of change. Teach what you've learned.

LIFE-ALTERING PRINCIPLE NO. 7— THE SLOW DEATH OF NOT BEING THE STAR—TAKEAWAYS

- Shift your focus away from time-consuming distractions and toward the pursuit of your personal goals
- Avoid the time sucks. Your life is at stake.
- There are only two ways to use your time—spend it or invest it.
- Stop obsessing and living vicariously through those you believe are "living the dream."
- It's easy to be a critic, but hard to be a creator.
- Focus your time and energy on becoming a star.
- The size of the stage is irrelevant.
- Rekindle your creative spirit and put something out there for the world to judge.
- If your plate is full, get a bigger plate—you can handle much more than you believe you can.

REALIZE PERMANENT, POSITIVE CHANGE—IN CLOSING

Please accept my sincere congratulations for completing your study of *The Seven Life-Altering Principles.*

Realizing permanent, positive change requires an incredible commitment. I applaud you for giving this your heart and soul and hope you find the rewards to be immense.

When you're ready, take a deep breath and move on to Part III, "Become Who You Were Born to Be."

The fun is just getting started.

PART III

BECOME WHO YOU WERE BORN TO BE

CHAPTER 14

WHAT IS YOUR *WHAT?*
AN INTRODUCTION

The ideal life is in our blood and never will be still. Sad will be the day for any man when he becomes contented with the thoughts he is thinking and the deeds he is doing—where there is not forever beating at the doors of his soul some great desire to do something larger; which he knows he was meant and made to do.

—Phillips Brooks, clergyman and author, 1835-1893

Some people call their *WHAT* a gift from God. Some say they were born with their *WHAT* and never had any doubt about it. Others say it took them a long time to figure it out, but they finally know what their *WHAT* is.

The *WHAT* I am referring to is the single most crucial element of your life that needs to be identified, defined, and fulfilled. Until your *WHAT* has been satisfied, you will roam the earth like an unsated vampire—constantly searching, and forever thirsting.

Your unfulfilled *WHAT* will affect you in a variety of unexpected ways. It could be the source of your high blood pressure, the reason why you never feel "good enough," the cause of your general sense of loathing when you wake up, or the impetus behind your efforts at self-sabotage.

Your *WHAT* can't be ignored. Until you unleash your *WHAT* and put it front and center for the world to benefit from, it will eat away at both your body and your emotional core.

The choice is yours: Succumb to your *WHAT*'s greatness, and to its power to elevate you to the heights of your true self so you can achieve your destiny or lie on your deathbed knowing you squandered your most sacred gift.

So, what exactly is your *WHAT?*

Your *WHAT* is your unique, innate talent. It's what comes most naturally to you and you'd happily do it without being paid a cent.

When you're engaged in your *WHAT*, time stands still, and there's nothing else you'd rather be doing.

Your *WHAT* reflects who you were born to be. It's inseparable from who you are. It's your gift. And if you use it well, it's your gift to the world.

THE CITY BOY MEETS THE COUNTRY

There are numerous ways to describe your *WHAT.* One of my all-time favorites can be found in the 1991 movie, *City Slickers.*

In this film, Mitch Robbins (played by Billy Crystal) takes a break from his busy Manhattan lifestyle to vacation at a dude ranch in the country in an effort to "find himself" and work his way

out of a mid-life funk. During his journey he meets Curly Washburn (played by Jack Palance), who represents everything Mitch is not: carefree, tough as nails, and—most importantly—centered.

I've seen hundreds of movies in my life, but only a handful really hit home. What stuck most in my mind from *City Slickers* was a scene that seemed oddly profound at the time, but I didn't take in its full meaning until years later.

It involves Curly and Mitch, each riding horseback, conversing about life. Curly is a tough, no-nonsense old cowboy who wears a black cowboy hat, red bandanna, black riding gloves, and always has a lit cigarette hanging precariously from the corner of his mouth. His voice sounds like it was passed down from Moses, and he talks with the confidence of a man who's seen it all.

In comparison, Mitch is a small, unassuming city guy who's wearing a New York Mets baseball cap, and a shirt and khakis that might have come from L.L. Bean. The best way to describe the difference between them is this eloquent comment Curly makes to Mitch earlier in the movie: "I crap bigger than you."

In the scene that had the greatest impact on me, Curly says, "You city folk, you worry about a lot of shit."

Mitch replies, "Shit?! My wife basically told me she doesn't want me around."

Curly chuckles. "Is she a redhead?"

"I'm just saying..."

Curly interrupts. "How old are you...38?"

"39."

"Yeah. You all come here at about the same age; with the same problems. Spend about 50 weeks a year getting knots in your rope, and then you think two weeks out here will untie them for you. None of you get it. Do you know what the secret of life is?"

"No, what?"

Curly smiles and holds up one finger: "This."

"Your finger?"

Still holding up one finger, Curly says, "One thing. Just one thing. You stick to that and everything else don't mean shit."

Mitch holds up his own finger. "That's great. But what's the one thing?"

Curly says, "That's what you've got to figure out..." And then he rides away.

Curly calls it "one thing." I call it your *WHAT.*

It doesn't matter what you call it. You just need to figure out what it is.

THE TWO CHOICES

If you have yet to identify your *WHAT*, you probably feel unfulfilled and as if life is passing you by. You have only two choices:

- Identify your *WHAT* and start living as your true self.
- Accept that your current vocation is your *WHAT*, live it as best you can, and quit complaining.

You might be thinking there's simply no way the second possibility is true. Spend the next 50 years flipping burgers and making fries? Absolutely not!

Well, maybe not flipping burgers until you retire. But if you grew up loving to cook, and seeing people eat good food inexpensively makes you happy, spending your life in the kitchen could be what you truly want.

For that matter, there have been a number of successful entrepreneurs who started out flipping burgers and ended up owning multiple fast-food restaurants that have earned millions.

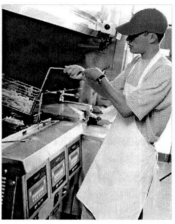

The point is, consider the possibility that what you're doing now is your *WHAT*. Some people zig and zag in their careers until they find their way, but others get on the right path early on and just take awhile to recognize and leverage it.

Identifying your *WHAT* isn't easy; and many resist the whole concept. I've had people respond with:

"How is it possible that someone has just one thing she overwhelmingly loves to do?"

"What if I don't have a *WHAT*?"

"Why should I spend my time figuring out what my *WHAT* is? My life is just fine."

It saddens me that most people neglect to dedicate the time required to find out who they are and what extra special gifts they possess.

Even sadder is that many of our world's best minds and most passionate souls have identified their *WHAT*, but live in situations that deprive them of the opportunity to realize their greatness.

If you're reading this from the comfort of an easy chair, a park bench on a beautiful day, or your favorite coffeehouse, count your blessings. Recognize that anything and everything you desire can be yours—because you possess the freedom and resources your country has to offer for pursuing your destiny.

Put away all excuses. Be grateful for the opportunities available to you.

And prepare yourself for a life-altering journey.

YOUR WHAT IS WAITING

Identifying your *WHAT* usually isn't easy. But there are three ways you can facilitate this quest.

1. *Schedule Time, and Grant Permission, to Learn About Yourself*

Devote focused, quiet time to identifying your *WHAT.* (Sometimes this is all it takes.)

It's a good idea to set aside a part of each day to get in touch with yourself and focus on what makes you tick.

This can be done in many ways. Some people find meditation or yoga to be effective in starting inner dialogues. Others may prefer a quiet walk in a park or time spent in a place of worship. Whatever is the right approach for you, begin scheduling time to do it.

If you've never tried this before, you'll soon realize that taking time out to listen to your inner self is one of the most valuable and satisfying things you can do.

2. *Let Go of Denial*

As explained in Chapter 5, you may have drifted so far from The Pinnacle that your life scarcely reflects your core identity. You may have even convinced yourself that you're a whole other person.

If the true you is buried beneath the emotional rubble of the past, it's time to dig deep and rescue it. Explore why you've chosen to deny yourself, and everyone else, the gift of who you really are; then do everything you can to become who you were born to be.

3. *Vigorously Explore Your Past*

When you were a toddler, you explored the world with unabashed curiosity. If you saw something that was of interest, you would be immediately drawn to it, and you'd pursue it unreservedly, without any worry about looking silly or what others thought.

Then you started being told "no." This was usually for your own good, such as the time you thought the oven was a TV. Still, you learned to avoid hearing "no," and that resulted in your taking fewer chances and only pursuing activities that you were confident would garner approval.

At some critical point, this may have led you to deny your true self and your natural gifts. If you believe this happened, think back and identify the point in your life when you took the wrong fork in the road.

And then reclaim your proper path and give yourself a second chance to live your *WHAT*.

These are merely the initial steps for discovering your *WHAT*. To probe further, proceed to the next chapter.

WHAT IS YOUR *WHAT?*
AN INTRODUCTION—TAKEAWAYS

- Your *WHAT* is a unique, innate talent that comes most naturally to you.
- When you're engaged in your *WHAT*, time stands still, and there's nothing else you'd rather be doing.
- Your *WHAT* reflects who you were born to be and is inseparable from who you are.
- You only have two choices: 1) Identify your *WHAT* or 2) Accept that your current vocation is your *WHAT*.
- Three ways to facilitate identifying your *WHAT*: 1) Grant yourself permission to find it. 2) Let go of denial. 3) Vigorously explore your past.

CHAPTER 15

THE THREE-STEP PROCESS OF IDENTIFYING YOUR *WHAT*

Take up one idea. Make that one idea your life—think of it, dream of it, live on that idea. Let the brain, muscles, nerves, every part of your body be full of that idea, and just leave every other idea alone. This is the way to success. That is the way great spiritual giants are produced.

—Swami Vivekananda, Indian spiritual leader, 1863-1902

In the previous chapter, you learned about the importance of your *WHAT* and were provided some initial suggestions for identifying it. This chapter continues the exploration in more depth, offering a three-step process for revealing this vital aspect of yourself.

I refer to this process as *The Seven Seeds of Your Soul*.

STEP ONE: THINGS YOU LOVE TO DO

To begin, find a quiet place where you can think. No TV. No radio. No iPod. No kids. Just you, alone with your thoughts.

If this feels uncomfortable, that could be part of the problem. It's hard to hear the inner you when you're continually distracted by background noise. So turn away from the distractions and focus on what's most important: the real you.

Now that you're in a place of silence, think about all the things you love to do. Whatever they are, write them down in the space that follows. Don't worry about anyone else reading your list; it's for you alone.

For example, most of us enjoy having sex. If that applies, write it down.

Maybe you love playing sports. And playing with your kids. If so, mark those down.

Think back. What did you enjoy as a teenager? Even if you haven't done something for years, if it would still bring you pleasure, write it down.

Focus on the activities and interactions that lift your soul. Avoid listing skills you're good at simply become you've practiced them over time (e.g., problem solving).

Dig even deeper. When you were a child, were you drawn to a certain cartoon or a certain book? What was your favorite toy? Think back to a time when you laughed hysterically—what triggered the laughter?

What's your earliest memory? Why do you think it's stuck with you when so many other memories have faded away?

As an adult, what gives you goose bumps? For me, it's witnessing someone's soul re-ignite. There is a specific moment when it all clicks and you can see a person's true self re-emerge. It's as if something immensely precious had been buried under years of pain, or chaos, or denial; then the key to the treasure chest is turned, and when the cover is opened—it all glows.

Maybe you get goose bumps when you hear a powerful singer belt out an incredible rendition of a song. Maybe it's when you pick up your child at school and his eyes light up with unbridled joy when he sees you. Maybe it's when you come up with a really good idea and you know you've found the solution you'd been looking for.

When recalling a special moment, try not to be too literal; look for the subtext. For example, let's say you have a fond memory of an evening spent bowling with your grandmother. Instead of writing "bowling with Grammy" on your list, broaden it to "spending time with a beloved family member."

As another example, let's say you closed a huge deal last year and felt really good about it. The monetary rewards are the tangibles. But what matters for this exercise is the sense of accomplishment you felt and how it enhanced your feeling of self-worth.

When you're ready, please create your list.

THINGS I LOVE TO DO:

_____

_____

_____

_____

_____

_____

_____

_____

_____

_____

_____

_____

_____

_____

_____

_____

_____

_____

_____

_____

_____

_____

_____

Look at your list. Did you miss something? Were you in denial about anything?

Try to add more items to the list. This is your life. Take inventory. And be completely honest.

If compiling this list takes a day to complete, so be it. If it takes a week, that's ok too. Whenever your list includes everything you feel it should, come back to finish this exercise.

The next step is to put the activities you've identified in order of preference. My list looked like this:

1. *Be intimate with my wife.*
2. *Spend time with my wife, kids, close friends, and close family members.*
3. *Help people live as their true selves.*
4. *Snuggle with my wife or kids.*
5. *Laugh and see people smile and laugh.*
6. *Listen to music, produce music and spin records.*
7. *See Lenny Kravitz perform.*
8. *Practice Brazilian Jiu-Jitsu.*
9. *Think strategically and creatively.*
10. *Be outside in the warm sun.*
11. *Achieve my goals and enjoy a sense of accomplishment.*
12. *Come up with ideas and launch new businesses.*
13. *Work with entrepreneurs to help develop their businesses.*
14. *Attend sporting events or other live performances.*
15. *Teach.*
16. *Mentor.*
17. *Get a really good massage.*
18. *Play golf.*
19. *Eat delicious food and enjoy a really good drink.*
20. *Dance.*
21. *Brainstorm.*
22. *Write.*
23. *Sleep late.*
24. *Work collaboratively with others.*
25. *Watch sports—basketball, football, and the Ultimate Fighting Championship—and other entertainment on TV.*
26. *Debate.*

This is what I mean about being honest. You're reading a book I wrote, and I'm listing writing as being way down at No. 22. I'm not a professional writer, but I couldn't be more fired up about the ideas I'm expressing, partly because they touch on Nos. 3, 9, 15, and 16.

I therefore hired several editors whose *WHAT*s are creating great books to go over my manuscript and make this book as concise, clear, and reader-friendly as possible.

I want you to be just as brutally honest, because actively seeking and accepting the truth is critical if you're going to find your *WHAT.*

You might be hesitant about admitting that you love to do something because you feel others won't approve. But if it's moral and legal, then why care what others think?

Stop trying to impress people you don't really like.

Stop getting along and start living.

Go back to your list. What didn't you write down that you know needs to be there? Return to your quiet place and dig really deep.

If you've been thoroughly honest with yourself, your *WHAT* now appears somewhere on your list.

Some have described identifying their *WHAT* as one of the most powerful feelings of their lives. If you can pinpoint your *WHAT,* it should feel like throwing a 500-pound bag of sand off your shoulders.

When you're ready, please organize your list in order of preference.

Things I Love To Do, in Order of Preference:

Step Two: Things You Hate to Do

The next step in the process of identifying your *WHAT* requires you to be totally honest about all the things you hate to do. If you're clear about what activities you despise, you can establish a strong foundation for moving your life forward by starting to let them go.

For example, maybe you abhor filing. You consider it mindless, time-consuming, unfulfilling work. And you always end up with a paper cut. Standing in front of a file cabinet with a 12-inch stack of paper to put away using some arcane system makes you want to light a match and set them on fire.

Whatever it is that pushes your buttons, write it down in the space that follows.

Also, reflect on why you deplore an activity. Did you see or experience something related to the activity that traumatized you as a child? Or that you were teased about as a teenager?

Did you do something when you were younger that so upset you—e.g., working at your family's slaughterhouse—that you swore to never do it again? And are you doing something similar now regardless?

What regular occurrences in your life make your blood curdle? Do you tell your boss how great he is, even though you'd like to kick him down a flight of stairs? Are you "friends" with the couple two houses down whom you can't stand simply because you don't want to have an inharmonious relationship with neighbors?

Whatever it is that eats at you, write it down. Even if you worry others might see it as petty, include it. This exercise takes place without judgment. The key is to acknowledge your thoughts and feelings.

When you're ready, please create your list.

THINGS I HATE TO DO:

_____

_____

_____

_____

_____

_____

_____

_____

_____

_____

_____

_____

_____

_____

_____

_____

_____

_____

_____

_____

_____

_____

_____

_____

_____

_____

_____

_____

_____

_____

You may be amazed at how freeing it is to get all this down on paper. Activities you perform regularly that you've never admitted deeply bother you will jump out and yell at you. Get it all out. Don't hold anything back.

As with Step One, take as much time as you need, whether it's a day or a week. What matters is getting it all down.

The next step is to put the activities you've identified in order from most distasteful to least. My list looked like this:

1. *Deal with minutiae.*
2. *Tolerate others' lack of integrity (e.g., people not honoring their commitments).*
3. *Have my feelings minimized or mitigated.*
4. *Witness oppression, racism, discrimination, suffering, and rudeness.*
5. *Be lied to, or lie to someone else.*
6. *Affect someone in a negative manner.*
7. *Hear people complain, even if they're justified.*
8. *Be yelled at.*
9. *Be treated poorly or unfairly.*
10. *Disappoint others by not delivering on my promises or projections.*
11. *Sit at a desk for a prolonged period of time.*
12. *Clean up other people's problems.*
13. *Deal with governmental or corporate bureaucracy.*
14. *Tell white lies to cover up other people's problems.*
15. *Be late or wait for others.*
16. *Pay bills or do accounting work.*
17. *Be awakened out of a solid slumber or have to wake up early.*
18. *Engage in any sort of office work.*
19. *Placate people for whom I have no respect.*
20. *Tolerate really bad music.*
21. *Waste even one meal on crappy food (even worse when I have to pay for it).*
22. *Open a supposedly good bottle of wine only to find it tastes horrible.*
23. *Deal with my inability to breathe through my nose.*

24. Deal with my lower back pain.
25. Deal with my tinnitus.
26. Clean toilets.

When you're ready, please organize your list in order of distaste from most distasteful to least.

Things I Hate To Do, in Order of Distaste:

_____

_____

_____

_____

_____

_____

_____

_____

_____

_____

_____

_____

_____

_____

_____

_____

_____

_____

_____

_____

_____

_____

_____

_____

_____

_____

_____

Now that it's all down on paper, take a closer look. Do all of the items ring true? Did you miss anything? Were you being completely honest?

There's an often-quoted saying: "If you stand for nothing, you will fall for anything." What you wrote down are the things you shouldn't tolerate, yet you probably "fall" for most of them frequently.

Think about how you spend a typical day and figure out how much time is devoted to these activities you despise.

Now understand that you have to stop doing most of these things. Because life is too short. And because they're slowly killing you.

> *Every minute you engage in an activity you abhor reduces your life expectancy by an equal amount of time.*

You're probably getting paid for doing a lot of these things. (Comedian Drew Carey once remarked: "I belong to a therapy group for people who hate their jobs. It's called everybody. And it meets in a bar.") But whatever money you're making probably isn't worth the cost to your happiness, health, and sense of identity.

Of course, letting go of these drags on your life can take time, especially if the apparent alternatives are even worse. In the short term, you can try to establish a frame of mind that lets you do these things with minimal discomfort. In the long term, however, you should strive for creative solutions that let you drop these activities for good.

One other thing to consider is how you've put up with these self-destructive activities for so long. Your inner self must have been crying out to you to stop, and you responded by slapping a muzzle on it.

When you tell your deepest self to "zip it" and find ways to rationalize your behavior, you risk committing great harm not only to yourself, but to others.

After all, isn't this how evil in the world takes place? People shut themselves off to what they know in their souls is right, and make up excuses to perform acts that horrify them on some level. And the more they do it, the bigger the excuses they create so they can live with the lies.

This is why it's imperative to listen to your gut.

> *When something shakes you to your core and your inner voice screams at you to stop, this is your true self sending a direct message. Pay attention. It's your soul calling you.*

To the extent that there's a devil and an angel in you, your rationalizing brain is the Devil (I call this the Voice of Conjecture) and your soul is the Angel.

Whether or not you listen to your soul will determine the quality of your existence. The list you just created came from your inner angel. Heed it.

STEP THREE: THE SEVEN SEEDS OF YOUR SOUL

This section is where your previous work pays off in helping to identify your *WHAT*. Please place your final lists of *Things I Love To Do* and *Things I Hate To Do* in front of you. You'll be referring to them frequently during this exercise.

Let's start with the top item on your list of *Things I Love To Do*. Read it out loud so you can really feel the words. Next, ask yourself each of the following six questions as it relates to the activity.

Each answer should be a definitive yes or no. Trust yourself and don't second-guess. Your first answer will almost always be right:

1. *Even if you didn't get paid a cent for it, would you still do this?*

2. *Would doing this inspire you every day?*

3. *Does doing this come as naturally to you as breathing?*

4. *Do you feel you've been given a special gift to do this?*

5. *Does time seem to stand still when you're engaged in this activity?*

6. *Can you possibly make money doing this?*

Often, people have difficulty answering *yes* or *no* to questions 4 and 6. For question 4, keep in mind that what you find appealing may be unappealing to others.

And while you may not yet be a master of this gift, the fact that you demonstrate interest in that activity qualifies as your being given a "special gift to do it." Therefore, your answer to question 4 would be *yes*.

As for question 6, your answer should reflect if you could *possibly* make money doing what you've identified—not whether or not you are currently making money doing so. Therefore, if you have an interest in, say, welding, but are not yet making money at it, your answer to question 6 would still be *yes*.

If any of your answers to these first six questions are *no*, please move on to the next item on your list of *Things I Love To Do*.

Again, read the item out loud, and then run it through the six questions.

Continue this process until you reach an item that prompts a *yes* to each of the six questions. When you arrive at the all *yes* item, ask yourself this final question:

7. *Does doing this involve anything on your list of Things I Hate To Do?*

As always, the goal is brutal honesty. To help make this clearer, let me walk you through what my process looked like.

As you may recall, the top item on my list of *Things I Love To Do* was:

Be intimate with my wife.

My answers to the first six questions were as follows:

1. *Even if you didn't get paid a cent for it, would you still do this?* **YES**
2. *Would doing this inspire you every day?* **YES**
3. *Does doing this come as naturally to you as breathing?* **YES**
4. *Do you feel you've been given a special gift to do this?* **NO**
5. *Does time seem to stand still when you're engaged in this activity?* **YES**
6. *Can you possibly make money doing this?* **NO**

It would be nice to think that I've been given a unique gift and could make money at it, but total honesty is required.

Therefore, I had to go to the next item on my *Love To Do* list, which is:

Spend time with my wife, kids, close friends, and close family members.

Again, I couldn't answer yes to all six questions, so I proceeded to the next item on my list:

Help people live as their true selves.

For this activity, my answers to the first six questions were as follows:

1. *Even if you didn't get paid a cent for it, would you still do this?* **YES**
2. *Would doing this inspire you every day?* **YES**
3. *Does doing this come as naturally to you as breathing?* **YES**
4. *Do you feel you've been given a special gift to do this?* **YES**

5. *Does time seem to stand still when you're engaged in this activity?* **YES**

6. *Can you possibly make money doing this?* **YES**

A clean sweep! All of those yes answers meant I could go on to the final question:

7. *Does doing this involve anything on your list of Things I Hate To Do?*

For each item on my *Hate* list, I read my beloved activity out loud first and then matched it against the despised activity.

Here were my answers:

1. *Deal with minutiae.* **NO**
2. *Tolerate others' lack of integrity (e.g., people not honoring their commitments).* **NO**
3. *Have my feelings minimized or mitigated.* **NO**
4. *Witness oppression, racism, discrimination, suffering, and rudeness.* **NO**
5. *Be lied to, or lie to someone else.* **NO**
6. *Affect someone in a negative manner.* **NO**
7. *Hear people complain, even if they're justified.* **YES**
8. *Be yelled at.* **NO**
9. *Be treated poorly or unfairly.* **NO**
10. *Disappoint others by not delivering on my promises or projections.* **NO**
11. *Sit at a desk for a prolonged period of time.* **NO**
12. *Have to clean up other people's problems.* **NO**
13. *Deal with governmental or corporate bureaucracy.* **NO**
14. *Tell white lies to cover up other people's problems.* **NO**
15. *Be late or having to wait for others.* **NO**
16. *Pay bills or doing accounting work.* **NO**

17. *Be awakened out of a solid slumber or have to wake up early.* **NO**

18. *Engage in any sort of office work.* **YES**

19. *Placate people for whom I have no respect.* **NO**

20. *Tolerate really bad music.* **NO**

21. *Waste even one meal on crappy food (even worse when I have to pay for it).* **NO**

22. *Open a supposedly good bottle of wine only to find it tastes horrible.* **NO**

23. *Deal with my inability to breathe through my nose.* **NO**

24. *Deal with my lower back pain.* **NO**

25. *Deal with my tinnitus.* **NO**

26. *Clean toilets.* **NO**

For the beloved activity to pass the final test of *The Seven Seeds of Your Soul*, it has to match no more than two of the hated activities. If you answer yes three or more times, you'll need to start the process again with the next item on your *Things I Love To Do* list.

You may wonder why I'm not insisting on a clean sweep. The fact is, in virtually anything you take on, there are going to be aspects of it you dislike doing. That's just reality. But the discomfort level has to be low enough to be tolerable.

By my being able to answer *yes* to the first six questions, and by answering *yes* no more than twice to the seventh question, I can conclude that No. 3 on my list satisfies the criteria of *The Seven Seeds*.

I then went on to review all 26 items on my *Things I Love* list to see if any other activity met all the criteria. As it turned out, only No. 3 did.

And this told me that *help people live as their true selves* is my *WHAT*.

Your review process should follow the same steps.

It's possible you'll come up with more than one item on your *Things I Love To Do* list that satisfies *The Seven Seeds of Your Soul*. If so, that's ok, as I'll explain later in this chapter.

This exercise may prove time-consuming if you've created an extremely long list (in which case, kudos for enjoying so many things), but it's well worth the investment. It's possible that your true calling doesn't appear in the first half or even the first two-thirds of your list, so be patient and work through every item.

Bottom line: This is flat-out the most important exercise in this entire book. Don't rush it. And no matter how long it takes, see it through to completion. Your life is at stake, and the rewards are incalculable.

Time to get to it!

After you've found your *WHAT*—or multiple *WHATs*—please write your results here:

1. _____

2. _____

3. _____

4. _____

If you've found a single *WHAT*, then you're done with this chapter and can proceed to Chapter 16, *Now That You've Found Your WHAT... Now What?!* If you've turned up multiple *WHATs*, please continue to the next section, *What If I Uncover More Than One WHAT?*

If, after going through the entire process, you've been unable to identify any activity that satisfies *The Seven Seeds of Your Soul* criteria, please return to the beginning of this chapter and start again... in a very quiet place, taking all the time you need.

Your *WHAT* is there for you to discover. Commit to this exercise and you'll find it.

WHAT IF I UNCOVER MORE THAN ONE **WHAT?**

It's common to come up with two, three, or even four *WHATs*. If this happened, it simply means you have more work to do in this process.

Please write down your *WHATs* again:

1. _____

2. _____

3. _____

4. _____

If you came up with more than four *WHATs*, chances are you weren't sufficiently honest during the process—for example, you may have created too short a list of things you hate to do. In this case, please return to the start of this chapter and try again.

Once you have four or fewer *WHATs*, look for synergies among them and ways you might either combine them into a single *WHAT* or pursue them all in ways that enhance each other.

For instance, if your *WHATs* are cooking and teaching, you can pursue becoming a master chef and, once you know enough, pass along what you've learned to aspiring chefs. You'll probably find you learn as much from your students as they do from you, so your teaching will ultimately make you an even better chef.

As another example, if your two *WHATs* are sports and writing, you're likely to be an excellent sports writer.

One of my participants in The Reinvention Workshop identified cooking, food, photography, and travel as her *WHATs*. After brainstorming with the class, we concluded that her *WHAT* is to become a traveling photographer who captures images of people enjoying the foods they love.

She is completely inspired by the idea and has begun putting the pieces in motion to realize her destiny. Talk about a dream job!

If the synergy between your *WHATs* isn't evident, or if you're unmoved by the *WHAT* you've discovered, you'll have to be more creative. You might even pursue *WHATs* on parallel tracks for a while to learn which draws you in the most.

Another strategy is to clarify who your audience is and identify a noun or two that ties your *WHAT*s together. Carol S. of Miller Beach, Indiana, another Reinvention Workshop participant, identified healing and teaching as her two *WHAT*s. While an excellent start, healing and teaching can be applied in myriad ways.

After exploring further, she recognized that her *WHAT* specifically involves healing and teaching the disadvantaged and the elderly. By adding two nouns to the equation, Carol's *WHAT* immediately became clear.

Mark Twain said: "The difference between the right word and the almost right word is the difference between lightning and the lightning bug." To make a meaningful difference, you'll eventually need to pinpoint what stirs your soul.

If you continue to have trouble identifying your *WHAT*, or understanding how to move forward with the discoveries you've made, enlist those in your closest circle. Often what's hardest for you to see is obvious to others.

Eventually, you'll find one *WHAT* that's your central passion. When you do, life as you know it will never be the same.

THE THREE-STEP PROCESS OF IDENTIFYING YOUR *WHAT*—TAKEAWAYS

- Stop trying to impress people you don't really like.
- If you stand for nothing, you'll fall for anything.
- Every minute you engage in an activity you abhor reduces your life expectancy by an equal amount of time.
- The quality of your existence is determined by whether or not you listen to your gut.
- Discover your *WHAT* by exploring The Seven Seeds of Your Soul.
- Become clear on who you were born to be.
- The world is waiting for you.

CHAPTER 16

NOW THAT YOU'VE FOUND YOUR *WHAT*... NOW WHAT?!

You were born to win. But to be a winner, you must plan to win, prepare to win, and expect to win.

—Hilary Hinton "Zig" Ziglar, author and motivational speaker

Identifying your *WHAT* may bring you a sense of purpose more powerful than you could have ever imagined. Life without purpose is frightening, yet most people drift along directionless, going wherever the road happens to take them.

Now that you've found your *WHAT*, your personal GPS resides at the forefront of your soul. It's there to call upon whenever you feel lost.

Envisioning your ideal destination is one of the most effective tools in your mental arsenal. Picture what living out your *WHAT* will look like on a daily basis. See yourself doing exactly what you truly want to be doing. Imagine basking in the glow of living your life to its fullest potential.

And see yourself getting paid. You deserve to not just eke out a living, but to reap extraordinary financial rewards for doing what you were born to do. That's one of the goals.

That said, it's unrealistic to instantly start a new career pursuing your *WHAT.* You'll first need to identify your niche, create a winning game plan, and begin a patient, but steady, transition.

HONE IT TO OWN IT!

George Washington Carver said: "If you can do a common thing in an uncommon way, you'll command the attention of the world." To become one-of-a-kind as opposed to one-of-many, it's imperative to create your own market, charge a premium for it, and have the world knocking down your door to benefit from your incredible talent.

Running in commodity-driven circles where price is king and service or originality means squat will inevitably lead to frustration. Your goal is to establish yourself as the only choice within your defined area of expertise.

By identifying your *WHAT*, you've taken the first step towards achieving greatness. Your long-term plan, however, is to implement a highly focused approach to identifying where you'll direct your energy.

Let's look at three examples that illustrate the importance of focus.

Café Du Monde in New Orleans is known for one item—beignets. A beignet (which is French for "doughnut") is a square piece of fried dough covered in powdered sugar. One order consists of three pieces and costs $2.36.

Established in 1862 in New Orleans' French Market, Café Du Monde is open 24 hours a day, seven days a week (with the exception of Christmas Day and the occasional hurricane). Its entire menu consists of beignets, dark roasted coffee and chicory, white and chocolate milk, fresh-squeezed orange juice and soft drinks.

By focusing on one ordinary thing (essentially a fancy doughnut) and producing it in an extraordinary manner, one simple, high-margin product has resulted in unparalleled success.

Allstar Electrical Services in Denver, Colorado has been in business since 2000 and has earned an A rating on Angie's List, the popular subscription-based website that aggregates consumer reviews of local service companies by trade and area. Allstar concentrates on residential and commercial work with a focus on repairs and remodeling.

"We're experts in electrical installation for residential and commercial jobs, both indoors and outdoors, and focus on remodeling and repairs," said owner Gary Stone. "We don't do framing, drywall, plumbing, heating, roofing or windows. We do electrical work and we do it better than anyone."

While the natural urge may be to expand his offerings to take on a broader scope of work, Stone resists such temptation by concentrating on what he does best—electrical work—and continues to grow his business as a result.

Sean Rich is the president and CEO of Tortuga Trading in Carlsbad, California. The company specializes in antique arms and armament from all over the world, concentrating on the 16th through 19th centuries. Talk about honing it!

Sean's love for the past began at age 10 when he acquired his first antique weapon. Over the years, he has participated in numerous archaeological digs;

Sean and pirates on set at Disney Studios

was designated as New Jersey's state representative for Gulf Coast Rare Coins and Investments where he specialized in treasure recovered from the Spanish Galleon Atocha and 1715 Plate Fleet; and underwent a master five-year apprenticeship for antique gun restoration while attending Salve Regina University in Newport, Rhode Island.

His expertise led to a three-year stint as a weapons consultant for Walt Disney Studios' Second Mate Productions. Their work includes the second and third *Pirates of the Caribbean* movies.

In 2009, Sean began working with Leftfield Productions, producers of The History Channel's *Pawn Stars*, as an antique arms and armament specialist. Whenever rare arms or armament from the 16th through 19th centuries show up at the pawn shop, there's only one person the owners need to call before making their purchase decision: Sean.

By becoming an expert in a specific field, he has created his own market, is able to charge a premium for it, and has the world knocking down his door to pay for what comes most naturally to him... his *WHAT.*

This is your goal. Do one thing, do it better than anyone else, and get paid extraordinarily well for your talent.

But to achieve this level of game-changing impact, you'll need to become intently cued in to what most appeals to your soul, then concentrate on the precise activities that drive you to make an inordinate difference. By recognizing that a broad-stroke approach results in career suicide, you'll begin to ask yourself the right questions and hone in on your niche.

Think about the most successful or happiest people you know—the lawyer who only takes on fathers' rights cases, the dentist who specializes in pediatric root canals, or the teacher who focuses on troubled teens.

They've all become experts in one specific arena, dedicated their lives to it, and are compensated at levels far superior to those of their counterparts. Getting to this point, however, is a journey.

It took me years to recognize that while personal development is my field of interest, my *WHAT* is helping people identify theirs.

Many doctors begin as general practitioners before deciding on their specialty. The majority of successful entrepreneurs endured multiple business failures before creating ventures that make the most of their passion.

You will undergo a similar process. Therefore, it's vital to begin pursuing the *WHAT* you've identified and take the next steps: creating your game-plan and entering the transition.

THE GAME PLAN

John Wooden is the greatest college basketball coach in history. As head coach of the UCLA Bruins from 1948 to 1975, Wooden led the Bruins to an unprecedented 10 NCAA titles, four perfect 30-0 seasons, and a record winning streak of 88 games.

Wooden attributes much of his success to his unwavering mantra:

> *"Failure to prepare is preparing to fail."*

As UCLA amassed victory after victory, Coach Wooden refused to rest on his laurels. He prepared a detailed game plan for each opponent while visualizing his intended outcome.

Every season, Coach Wooden's ultimate objective was to win the national championship. This required his team to be victorious as often as possible during the regular season and to win each tournament game. It also meant that each individual player had to outperform his counterpart.

His players understood this. They recognized that the result of each play had meaningful impact on whether or not UCLA would win the NCAA Championship.

In other words, they all stayed focused on their ultimate objective and took steps on a day-by-day and moment-by-moment basis to achieve it.

You should adopt a similar strategy in pursuit of your *WHAT*. In order to reach the top of the mountain, there are three critical steps you'll need to take.

STEP ONE: IDENTIFY YOUR ULTIMATE OBJECTIVE

Imagine what living your *WHAT* will look and feel like. The more vividly you can create a mental scene of living your *WHAT*, the more likely you'll be to realize it.

As Steve Jobs asks: "How will you leave your dent on the world?" Be clear on your Ultimate Objective and maintain laser-like focus on making it happen.

Add details to the scene by asking yourself questions such as:
- In what city are you based?
- Do you travel? If so, how often?

- Do you work from home as a sole proprietor, or in a large office with hundreds of colleagues?
- Do you have employees who report to you? If so, approximately how many?
- How much money do you make?
- Are you famous?
- How large is your audience?
- Who are your clients?
- How are you going to recreate your *WHAT* in an extraordinary way?

Think about what's most important to you, and in the space that follows, detail your Ultimate Objective:

_____
_____
_____
_____
_____
_____
_____
_____
_____
_____
_____
_____
_____
_____

Step Two: Identify the Steps that Lead to Your Ultimate Objective

Pursuing your *WHAT* may seem like an overwhelming task. Breaking the process down into small steps you can readily envision will make it feel more concrete and achievable.

By way of example, after discovering her *WHAT*, a participant in The Reinvention Workshop identified her Ultimate Objective as teaching a spirituality writing class. We defined the steps required to reach that goal as:

   a. Establish her niche and hook—that is, her unique offering.

   b. Take classes, research what others are doing, intern, and imitate those she admires.

   c. Write the first sentence of her book and/or classroom materials.

   d. Enlist trusted sources to review her plan and provide feedback and support (monetary or emotional).

   e. Create her classroom materials and website.

   f. Clarify her audience (e.g., who will attend, ideal number of participants, costs to create the class, etc.)

   g. Secure the venue.

   h. Rehearse her presentation.

   i. Market her class via her website, Facebook, Twitter, fliers, a public relations campaign, networking, advertising, and sponsors.

   j. Register participants.

   k. Prepare the venue.

   l. Begin her class.

Can you develop a comprehensive plan now that will remain effective in every aspect years from now? Of course not, because the other side of the coin is John Lennon's famous observation:

> ### *"Life is what happens while you are busy making other plans."*

Just because life is unpredictable doesn't mean you shouldn't have plans, though. It simply means that you should be flexible and adaptable, and always ready to change your game plan in response to the unexpected.

With this in mind, I want you to identify the steps that lead to your Ultimate Objective. Your final goal, naturally, is to reach it. Therefore, please show your Ultimate Objective on the first line and work backward to identify the first step, which should be something you can begin doing today.

Many find that working backward is easier than starting with today. If you prefer to start with today and work forward, that's ok too.

If this process makes zero sense and you're too overwhelmed to start, I'd encourage you to put down *Journey To You* and embrace all the ways the world is eager to help. Buy books on your subject matter, take classes, hire a coach, intern, join a free group, and/or apprentice yourself to a mentor.

And use the Internet. It offers information on almost anything you can think of—there are even free online videos on how to break into most major professions. Someone who's already living out your *WHAT* is probably writing a free blog and selling a newsletter, book, or DVD full of helpful information.

The bottom line is that you're not reinventing the wheel. Find someone who is doing what you want to do and shadow them until you figure out their process.

Once you're ready to identify the steps required to reach your Ultimate Objective, please do so in the space that follows. Obviously, this will not be your final version. It will, however, provide an outline for what lies ahead and inspire you to reach your Ultimate Objective by breaking the process down into bite-sized, manageable pieces.

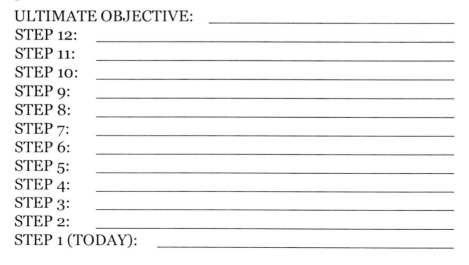

ULTIMATE OBJECTIVE: _____
STEP 12: _____
STEP 11: _____
STEP 10: _____
STEP 9: _____
STEP 8: _____
STEP 7: _____
STEP 6: _____
STEP 5: _____
STEP 4: _____
STEP 3: _____
STEP 2: _____
STEP 1 (TODAY): _____

Becoming who you were born to be requires significant effort. Having some sense of the path you'll be traveling will help you prepare for whatever you might face along the way.

By defining the steps required to reach your Ultimate Objective, you shift the odds of it actually happening in your favor.

STEP THREE: BEGIN

This may sound easy enough, but I can't over-emphasize its importance. All the planning in the world is worthless until you start acting on those plans.

By simply taking your first baby step toward achieving your Ultimate Objective, you have taken a monumental leap forward... and have now entered The Transition.

THE TRANSITION

While finding your *WHAT* and creating your game plan are crucial turning points, you won't magically turn into a master of your chosen field. The transition to living your *WHAT* takes time.

It's within this period of advancing from where you are now to where you want to be that you'll make yourself humble and vulnerable, take risks, learn your trade, hone your skills, and solidify your understanding of what it means to live out your *WHAT* on a daily basis.

Your transition will be a work in progress. It's not unusual to modify a life plan several times over as you move from your mental destination to reality.

Be patient as you learn and develop your skills. Meanwhile, don't quit your day job. Earn while you learn. Then gradually begin shifting your schedule to invest more and more time on your *WHAT*.

> **While working toward your WHAT,**
> **you may be pleasantly surprised at how**
> **issues that once bothered you lose much**
> **of their impact.**

I liken the transition to an evolving recipe. Today, your recipe comprises 100 parts current vocation and 0 parts *WHAT*.

After you take the first step toward realizing your *WHAT*, your recipe shifts to 99.9 parts current vocation and 0.1 parts *WHAT*. By staying focused on your Ultimate Objective and working diligently to bring your vision to fruition, you'll eventually reach 100 parts *WHAT* and 0.0 parts current vocation.

As an example, if becoming a doctor is your Ultimate Objective, your mix shifts to favoring your *WHAT* the closer you get to graduation. Once you've secured a position as a full-time doctor and 100 percent of your income is derived from the fulfillment of your *WHAT*, you have completed the transition.

Of course, some *WHAT*s are tougher to transition to than others. If your *WHAT* is to be a Hollywood film director, it may seem like you have an impossible task in front of you.

Keep thinking to yourself "I'm possible" and maintain a positive frame of mind. It's amazing how, once you know your purpose and discuss your intentions with others, you can surmount what appears to be insurmountable.

Nothing worthwhile comes easy. You may need to intern, take on whatever jobs you can to pay the bills, and sacrifice to get there. However, as Dave Ramsey, author of *The Total Money Makeover* and nationally syndicated radio host says: "If you will live like no one else, later you can live like no one else."

Stay focused on your game plan, talk to everyone you know about it, latch onto a mentor (or two) and you'll be like a locomotive on a downhill track. Nothing will stop you unless you step on the brakes.

And while it will take considerable effort and commitment to achieve your Ultimate Objective, remember that the pain is only temporary. Fulfilling your *WHAT* as your full-time vocation is now in sight. Commit to making it happen, and in time, it absolutely will.

A *Final Thought* on *Your* WHAT

Every year *Parade* magazine publishes a cover story titled "What People Earn." The article showcases a cross-section of people and professions across the country, listing what they do for a living and how much they earn.

They do a good job of presenting a snapshot of America from an employment and demographic standpoint. The results are shocking.

While a farmhand in Iowa might make $25,000 a year, a professional tennis player could be pulling down $35 million.

What's intriguing to me is that the people making the most money are those about whom others might say, "They're not working very hard."

Famous actors, great athletes, acclaimed CEOs, and other stars actually put in a tremendous number of hours to master their professions. But to those who break their backs to make $25,000 a year, those at the top often appear to be having a picnic in the park and getting paid a fortune to do so.

And therein lies the beauty of pursuing your *WHAT*. Work should be fun and you should be paid extraordinarily well for your contributions.

Ultimately, your goal is for your work to directly reflect your true self. When this happens, what you may perceive as an avocation will become your vocation. And your life will become a vacation.

Are you ready?

NOW THAT YOU'VE FOUND YOUR *WHAT*... NOW WHAT?!—TAKEAWAYS

- You deserve to reap extraordinary financial rewards for doing what you were born to do.
- "Failure to prepare is preparing to fail." – former UCLA basketball coach John Wooden
- "How will you leave your dent on the world?" – Apple CEO Steve Jobs
- Three critical steps to reach the mountaintop: 1) Identify your Ultimate Objective. 2) Define the steps that lead to your Ultimate Objective. 3) Begin.
- "Life is what happens while you are busy making other plans." – John Lennon
- Someone has already forged the path for you—follow it.
- Discuss your game plan with others.
- "If you will live like no one else, later you can live like no one else." – Dave Ramsey
- Turn what you may perceive as an avocation into your vocation—and get ready for life to become a vacation.

PART IV

FORGE YOUR PATH—
CREATE YOUR LEGACY

CHAPTER 17

PUTTING IT ALL TOGETHER

As a single footstep will not make a path on the earth, so a single thought will not make a pathway in the mind. To make a deep physical path, we walk again and again. To make a deep mental path, we must think over and over the kind of thoughts we wish to dominate our lives.

—Henry David Thoreau, writer and philosopher, 1817-1862

If you've patiently worked your way through the previous chapters, I hope you've experienced an incredible journey. You should now have a profoundly better understanding of who you are and what to do with your life.

That said, there are three more components to tackle in *JOURNEY TO YOU*. Using the exercises you've already performed, you'll create three personal references: your *Coat of Arms,* your *Letter of Reflection*, and *My Journey*.

These will provide visual summaries of the goals you've identified. Looking over these tools periodically will help you stay on point as you pursue becoming who you were born to be.

Let's begin by creating your *Coat of Arms.*

COAT OF ARMS: AN OVERVIEW

Coats of Arms date back to 12th century Europe. A knight's face was hidden by his visor during battle, so unique markings were created outside the coat of chain mail to make it easy to identify his nationality and lineage. This became known as his coat of arms.

While you may never need to do physical battle, life is full of attacks from others, as well as your own attempts at self-sabotage. To stay the course, it's helpful to have a "shield" that clearly defines your life's priorities and purpose. It's designed to repel anyone—including obsolete aspects of yourself—who seeks to prevent you from achieving your objectives. Your Coat of Arms will be this shield.

Let's take a look at a typical Coat of Arms heraldry.

Across the top:
SLOGAN or SECONDARY
MOTTO

On top of the Shield:
CORONET
MANTLING
HELM
WREATH
CREST

Left and right of the Shield:
SUPPORTERS

In the center:
SHIELD
(divided into sections)

Above the Motto:
ORDER and
COMPARTMENTS

At the bottom:
MOTTO

Across the top of the heraldry is what's known as the Slogan (also referred to as the Secondary Motto, Battle Cry, or War Cry).

Beneath the Slogan are the Coronet (or crown), the Mantling, the Helm (helmet), the Wreath (which sits above the Helm and is used to hold the Mantle in place), and the Crest (which sits atop the Helm).

In this exercise we'll focus on the Mantling, which shields the rear of the Helm, protecting the back of the head and neck from unseen attacks.

To the left and right of the Shield are Supporters. They're vital components that "hold together" the Shield.

In the center is the Shield, which can be divided into any number of sections, represented in various shapes and adorned with Common Charges (decorative elements in the form of words or symbols).

Beneath the Shield are the Order and the Compartments. The Order is a decorative feature of the Shield that typically represents an award granted to the bearer by the government or a religious body. The Compartments represent the design element placed under the Shield that the Supporters are pictured standing upon.

The final element is the Motto, which is a key phrase describing the overall intention of the bearer.

The next section will teach you how to use these ancient elements to represent the core values of your life.

CREATING YOUR COAT OF ARMS

The following are the five key areas you'll focus on for the creation of your Coat of Arms:

a. *Motto*

b. *Slogan*

c. *Mantling*

d. *Supporters*

e. *Shield*

(If a visual aid would be helpful, please refer to my completed Coat of Arms on page 215.)

MOTTO

Let's start with your Motto. Its job is to clearly state your life's overall purpose.

Your Motto should be bold, inspirational, possibly even spiritual, grounding you when everything else is out of whack. In one declarative sentence, it should summarize how you want to live your life and serve as an intrapersonal beacon.

Your Motto is your internal mantra. It's what you tell yourself to stay focused.

Please take some time to review your answers to previous exercises in this book and to quietly reflect on a sentence that sums them up. Jot down a few of your thoughts here:

_____

_____

_____

_____

To give you an example, my Motto is "Let Love Rule," the title of Lenny Kravitz's debut album and title track. In this song, he powerfully drives home a message of inspiration that moves me on a daily basis. When I've gotten sidetracked and lost sight of my primary goal, this Motto has been invaluable in putting me back on course.

I apply it to my behavior with my wife and children, with my friends, and even with business associates. It's with this Motto in mind that I find consistency and direction.

Creating your Motto is one of the most valuable things you can do. Please take the time to create a Motto that will have a substantial impact on you, both now and for years to come.

Once you've crafted your Motto, please write it here:

_____

_____

_____

SLOGAN

The next element on your Coat of Arms is your Slogan. While your Motto is effectively your spiritual mantra, your Slogan guides your interactions with others and clarifies how you want the world to perceive you. Often it is more detailed than one's Motto, but it should be concise enough to be memorable and effective.

After one look at your Slogan, you should have a clear understanding of your guiding interpersonal principles.

Please take some time to think about what would work well as your Slogan. Jot down a few of your thoughts here:

_____

_____

_____

_____

As an example, my Slogan is "Be Vulnerable. Be Authentic. Be a Positive, Motivating Influence."

This Slogan drives how I interact with people. It helps ensure that I'm clear, honest, and upbeat.

Once you've decided on your Slogan, please write it here:

_____

_____

_____

MANTLING

Next, create your Mantling, which shields the back of your head from unseen attacks.

Your Mantling represents what you depend on for protection. It "always has your back," repelling threats that you might not even notice.

This could be your family, your best friend, your belief in God, or choosing to live your life with kindness. It's whatever provides you with the peace of mind of knowing someone—or something—is in your corner.

Please take some time to ponder what would be appropriate for your Mantling. Jot down a few of your thoughts here:

_____

_____

_____

_____

_____

My Mantling consists of my wife and my boys. I would take a bullet for any of them, and each of them would do the same for me and for each other.

The idea is that you shouldn't embark on your journey all alone. Take along someone—or something—you trust with your life.

Once you've identified the elements of your Mantling, please write them here:

_____

_____

_____

Supporters

You're now ready to create your Supporters. Supporters are the people to whom you can consistently turn for honest, constructive feedback, and for keeping you focused on your goals. I call them *accountability partners.*

You can represent your Supporters figuratively (e.g., as lions or hearts), or literally, by using photos. Either way, they're the people who help you stay in touch with reality.

Be warned: It can be destructive to ask a friend or colleague to take on this role if he or she isn't going to be good at it. It's typically best to give this job to a peer who's facing similar challenges, or a loved one who you inherently trust, so you can share insights with each other as you both proceed on your journeys.

Please consider those in your life who are your most effective Supporters. Jot down a few of your thoughts in the space that follows:

_____

_____

_____

_____

_____

The Supporters in my life are my wife, Lena, and my good friend Symeon. I can always count on each of them to keep me honest, to challenge me and to maintain a strong focus on my objectives. I consider myself very lucky that my wife is an incredible accountability partner.

Who are your key Supporters? Of these people, which two can you most strongly depend on to be your accountability partners?

Symeon, his wife, Robin, Lena and me

Once you've decided, please write their names here:

_____

_____

SHIELD

The final element of your Coat of Arms is your Shield. For this exercise, divide the Shield into five sections that represent key areas of your life.

Your Shield should express your life's purpose. It can also include life-altering principles that have had a profound impact on you. It can be a mix of words and images.

Please consider what would most effectively prompt you to remember and stick to your life's goals. Jot down a few of your thoughts here:

_____

_____

_____

_____

My Shield contains these five sections:

1. At the top: "Helping People Live as Their True Selves."
2. In the center left: The words "Lines in the Sand" in a circle with a line diagonally through it.
3. In the center right: A music note.
4. In the lower left: A picture of my family.
5. In the lower right: "My Life. My Choice."

Creating my Shield took time and required several revisions. Expect to take some time with yours and to play around with it until it feels right.

That said, decide on the components of your Shield that you'd like in your first draft, and please write them on the following five lines:

1. _____
2. _____
3. _____
4. _____
5. _____

You're now ready to apply all of the choices you've made to your heraldry. First, please compile your answers here:

MOTTO: _____

SLOGAN: _____

MANTLING: _____

SUPPORTERS: _____

SHIELD:

1. _____

2. _____

3. _____

4. _____

5. _____

Finally, take your answers and insert them into their respective places using the blank template that follows.

I recommend not writing on the original template, but instead making multiple copies of the page. Better yet, download the Coat of Arms template from my website at SteveOlsher.com. Either way, with an unlimited number of blank templates, you'll be able to revise your Coat of Arms whenever you want.

For the Mantling, write your choices inside the body of the leaves to the left and right of the Helm.

For your Supporters, write their names inside the bodies of the lions or alongside the lions' tails.

For example, my completed Coat of Arms looks like this:

Please use this template to complete your Coat of Arms:

Once you've finished, let me be the first to offer my congratulations.

You now have your very own Coat of Arms. I hope you find it to be an inspirational tool. Display your Coat of Arms, refer to it periodically, and see how it fits.

Whenever you feel like changing any of its elements, don't hesitate to do so. Your Coat of Arms should be a fluid, organic document that reflects what's happening in your life.

You've covered a lot of ground in *JOURNEY TO YOU*. Use your Coat of Arms as a concise, visual reference to help you maintain focus on your new path.

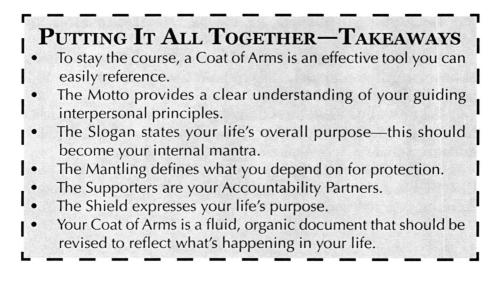

PUTTING IT ALL TOGETHER—TAKEAWAYS

- To stay the course, a Coat of Arms is an effective tool you can easily reference.
- The Motto provides a clear understanding of your guiding interpersonal principles.
- The Slogan states your life's overall purpose—this should become your internal mantra.
- The Mantling defines what you depend on for protection.
- The Supporters are your Accountability Partners.
- The Shield expresses your life's purpose.
- Your Coat of Arms is a fluid, organic document that should be revised to reflect what's happening in your life.

CHAPTER 18

WRITING YOUR LETTER OF REFLECTION

To accomplish great things, we must not only act, but also dream; not only plan, but also believe.

—Anatole France, winner of the Nobel Prize for Literature, 1844-1924

This book was truly a labor of love. I spent thousands of hours over a 26-month period writing, editing, and rewriting it. There are very few things that I've ever felt so compelled to create or that have provided me with such satisfaction.

The impetus for writing JOURNEY TO YOU started with a visit to my stepfather in the hospital which forced me to face my own mortality. A vision of my funeral flashed before my eyes, and the words I could hear being spoken over my grave were: "Here lies Steve Olsher. He devoted his life to chasing the almighty dollar."

It was a huge wake-up call that slammed me with the same force as a kick to the head. I suddenly realized that aside from family and friends, the only one who substantially benefited from my existence was me, me, and—did I mention?—me.

I began to think about how to best use the 35-40 years I had left and started wondering what accomplishments I could look back on toward the end of my life that would make me feel proud. Interestingly, none of them involved making money.

While I've enjoyed moderate success as an entrepreneur, it became clear that everything I've done as a professional was focused on profit.

I'd like to think that my real estate developments provide comfortable places for people to live and work. But if I were to die tomorrow, my tenants wouldn't be lining up to pay their final respects. They'd simply want to know where to send their rent check.

Liquor.com, which I co-founded in 2008, is an awesome website if you're looking for an expert guide to cocktails and spirits.

But there are thousands of online resources that offer sweet deals and niche-focused information.

My aim is to have a more meaningful impact on the world.

Writing this book, creating and facilitating The Reinvention Workshop and, I hope, helping you find your destiny is my way of heeding that call. Though it took some time to get here, as Sheldon J. Plankton on *SpongeBob SquarePants* says, "I can deny it no longer!"

What I now realize is that there's a significant difference between living well and living for the sake of making money. Don't get me wrong; as I've said, each of us is entitled to make a great living. I'm not one of those people who would suggest you resign yourself to life as a starving artist simply because you're compelled to draw.

What I am saying is that we're all obligated by our common bond of humanity to not only pursue what brings us financial success, but what also makes a positive impact on our community, our environment, and our world.

With this in mind, on December 23, 2008, I wrote my Letter of Reflection. My goal was to envision a life I'd be proud to remember in my final days.

Completing my Letter of Reflection has revitalized my sense of purpose. It concisely sums up what I want to accomplish between the day I wrote it and the day I leave this world.

Writing your own Letter of Reflection is a highly effective way to face your mortality, realize your time on this planet is limited, and provide you with direction and motivation to achieve the goals dearest to you. As Stephen Covey, author of *The 7 Habits of Highly Effective People*, said, "You must begin with the end in mind."

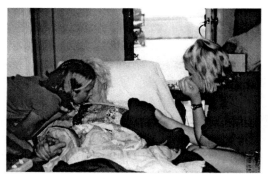

Take a few quiet moments to imagine yourself in your final days. Now ask yourself these questions:

- How do I feel about the life I lived?
- Am I happy about how my life affected the world?
- Did my life have the meaning I intended?
- Did I accomplish the things most important to me?
- When I imagine the people visiting me in my final days, do I sense they feel real loss, or are they there simply because they feel obligated?

If you were to die today, chances are most of your answers wouldn't be positive.

The good news is, you're still alive. And while tomorrow isn't a given, you can immediately begin constructing the life you desire and take full advantage of however many years are left to you.

First, try to identify all the things you most want to accomplish. Look through your answers to this book's exercises—including your Coat of Arms—for inspiration.

Now answer these questions:

1. What and/or who is most important to you?

_____

_____

2. What is your Motto?

_____

_____

3. What is your Slogan?

_____

_____

4. What did you identify as your life's purpose on your Shield?

_____

_____

5. How do you want to be remembered by those who knew you best?

_____

_____

_____

6. How do you want to be remembered by those who knew you only by name?

_____

_____

_____

7. What are you committed to accomplishing before you die?

_____

_____

_____

8. What principles, processes, and/or skills are you committed to mastering?

_____

_____

_____

9. What did you identify as your *WHAT*?

_____

_____

_____

10. In one sentence, to what will you dedicate your life from this point forward?

_____

_____

_____

To become who you were born to be, it's essential to create goals and objectives that serve to both anchor you from diversions and steer you toward your destiny.

You've had an incredible journey thus far. You've mastered *The Four Stages of Learning, The Vortex of Vulnerability, The Vortex of Invincibility,* and *The Pinnacle.* You've lived *The Seven Life-Altering Principles.* You've discovered your *WHAT.* And you've created your Coat of Arms.

With these in mind, write your Letter of Reflection in the space that follows. Begin with the end in mind. Everything else will fall into place.

_____

_____

_____

_____

_____

_____

_____

_____

_____

_____

_____

_____

_____

_____

_____

_____

_____

_____

_____

_____

_____

_____

_____

_____

_____

If you've completed your Letter of Reflection, I hope it proved illuminating to create. Refer to it whenever you feel adrift as it serves as a powerful guide to realizing your desired future.

Consider what you've written a first draft. It's a good idea to revise your Letter of Reflection periodically—once a year or so—to reflect changes in your life. If you keep each draft, you'll end up with a fascinating record of your process of transformation and how your hopes and dreams evolved over time.

Writing Your Letter of Reflection— Takeaways

- There's a significant difference between living well and living for the sake of making money.
- We're all obligated by our common bond of humanity to pursue things that have a positive impact on our community, our environment, and our world.
- Your Letter of Reflection provides a sense of purpose and helps define what you hope to accomplish between now and the end of your life.
- As Stephen R. Covey said, "You must begin with the end in mind."
- Pursue living as your true self and you'll achieve your true destiny.

CHAPTER 19

A FINAL WORD

I cannot give you a map. I can give you only a great passion to discover.
Yes, a map is not needed; great passion, great desire to discover is.
Then, I leave you alone and you go on your own.

—Bhagwan Shree Rajneesh, Indian spiritual leader, 1931-1990

Horace Mann, the 19th century politician and education advocate said, "We should be ashamed to die until we have made some major contribution to mankind."

How are you going to leave your mark? What will your contribution be?

The reality is that you're just a blip in time in a constantly transforming universe. But you do have the capacity to make an extraordinary difference in both the lives of those who share these moments with you and provide benefit for generations to come.

While you transition toward becoming who you were born to be, remember that those who have made their mark—people like Richard Branson, Sam Zell, Sean Combs, or Mother Teresa—all began just like you.

None were born with silver spoons in their mouths. Their journey began by taking the first step and by consistently choosing paths most congruent with who they are.

Virgin founder Richard Branson started by selling one record at a time through a mail-order business. Real estate and media tycoon Sam Zell convinced one landlord to let him manage his building. Entertainment mogul Sean Combs interned at Uptown

Records before becoming an executive, and eventually, releasing his first album. Mother Teresa sought to bring comfort to one person in need.

Each experienced hardship. Each experienced failure. Each persevered. None of them started out as who you know them to be.

To attain meaningful satisfaction and contentment, heed the words of Buddha: "It is better to travel well than to arrive." This is an essential mindset for cultivating ultimate achievement.

> ## Remember, the destination is the road. The journey is the destination.

Savor each step along your new path.

ONE LAST EXERCISE—MY JOURNEY

Finally, I'd like for you to reflect on your process of reinvention. Livng life in a powerful manner requires that you choose to live powerfully. My hope is that you are now fully committed to doing so.

You have invested significant time, energy, and emotion into becoming who you were born to be. I want you to realize an enormous return on your investment.

By completing this exercise and then declaring your commitment to achieving your desired objectives while having someone close to you witness and memorialize your declaration, the likelihood of realizing your goals is exponentially greater.

This final exercise provides a synopsis of your efforts and should be used as a personal guide to help maintain focus. I encourage you to remove the completed pages and post them in clear sight. (Additional forms can be found at SteveOlsher.com.)

When you're ready, please begin.

My Journey

1.   I am clear that I am prone to "lose it" when:

_____

2.   When faced with similar situations in the future, I will choose to:

_____

3.   These three moments have had a major impact on my life:

       a. _____

       b. _____

       c. _____

4.   I have internalized these moments to mean that I am:

_____

_____

5.   But, in fact, I am:

_____

_____

6.   I have identified my disconnects as:

_____

_____

7.   I choose to repair these disconnects by:

_____

_____

8.   Time absolutely stands still for me when I'm:

_____

_____

9.   Three people that I admire are:

_____

_____

_____

10.   I admire them because:

_____

_____

_____

11.   I have been most proud of myself when I:

_____

_____

12.   I believe I was able to excel in these moments because:

_____

_____

13.   I choose the following people to comprise my Circle of Four:

_____

_____

_____

_____

14.   I will seek to master:

_____

_____

15.   I have identified my *WHAT* as:

_____

_____

16.   The first step I am going to take to realize my *WHAT* is:

_____

_____

17.   Before I die, I want to:

_____

_____

_____

18.   The legacy I choose to leave is:

_____

_____

_____

_____

I, _____, on this _____ day
of _____, 20____, declare that I will no longer be driven
by my past; that I choose to reinvent my life; that I will absolutely
become who I was born to be no matter the circumstances; and that
I will forge my own path and create my desired legacy.

_____

Signature   Witness

THE END OF OUR JOURNEY TOGETHER

Bravo for completing JOURNEY TO YOU! Reinventing who you are and living as your true self are incredible accomplishments.

This journey has required you to explore the very depths of your being. You may have experienced some discomfort, and even pain, along the way as you shed self-destructive habits. I applaud you for sticking with it.

By completing this book and pursuing what you've learned, I'm confident that you'll enjoy profound and long-lasting, positive change.

I'd love to learn how JOURNEY TO YOU affected you. Please visit my website at SteveOlsher.com and send me an email to share your experiences.

My website provides free downloadable templates for creating your Pinnacle Pyramid, Vitality Curve, Coat of Arms, and more.

Additional online tools include interviews with people living their *WHAT*, podcasts, excerpts from my blog, free exercises and chapters from JOURNEY TO YOU, and my schedule for speaking and presenting The Reinvention Workshop, Hone It to Own It!, and What Is Your *WHAT*?

Lastly, I ask you to consider the words of motivational speaker Les Brown:

> **"Most people fail in life not because they aim too high and miss, but because they aim too low and hit."**

And some people never aim at all.

I encourage you to aim as high as you can imagine... and then aim higher. Commandeer life by living like a sniper. Don't just endeavor to hit the target—aim for the center of the bull's eye.

The world is waiting for you.

A FINAL WORD—TAKEAWAYS

- "We should be ashamed to die until we have made some major contribution to mankind."– Horace Mann
- How are you going to leave your mark? What will your legacy be?
- Becoming who you were born to be begins with taking the first step.
- To cultivate ultimate achievement, heed the words of Buddha: "It is better to travel well than to arrive."
- Living life in a powerful manner requires that you choose to live powerfully.
- Declare your commitment to achieve your desired objectives in front of a witness. Doing so exponentially increases the likelihood of realizing your goals.
- Commandeer life by living like a sniper. Don't just endeavor to hit the target—aim for the center of the bull's eye.

NOTES

Page 10—Windsock photograph courtesy of: http://www.grasmenre. co.nz/gallery/farm.asp

Page 11—Path to Freedom and Light painting by Karen Leroch. More information can be found at: http://www.karins-art.blogspot.com

Page 12—Four Stages of Learning diagram courtesy of: www.think-differently.org/2007_05_01_archive.html

Page 18—Man screaming photograph courtesy of: http:// images.sodahead.com/polls/000534253/polls_Man_screaming____ iStock_2541_305522_answer_1_xlarge.jpeg

Page 19—Embarrassed chimpanzee photograph courtesy of: http:// myfavoritesquadron.mlblogs.com/Embarrassed-Chimpanzee-Pre-Matted-C11774369.jpg

Page 20—Disconnected phone photograph courtesy of: http://4.bp.blogspot.com/_HXBKPv_qTFo/RzJjHztoNBI/ AAAAAAAAGAQ/5hKam7tnoaU/s400/disconnected.jpg

Page 23—Who Am I? photograph courtesy of: http://www.stritch. luc.edu/depts/facadvisory/YEAR%20I%20Info/Who%20Am%20I%20 pic.jpg

Page 26—Liar photograph courtesy of: http://blackgirlinthecity. files.wordpress.com/2009/11/liar-main_full.jpg

Page 27—Sad face photograph courtesy of: http://media. photobucket.com/image/sad%20face/edricke/sad_face.jpg

Page 29—Intersecting highways photograph courtesy of: http:// www.welove-music.com/blog/wp-content/uploads/2010/01/burtynsky_ losangeles.jpg

Page 31—Flower photograph courtesy of: http://www. williammillerhouse.com/blog/wp-content/uploads/2010/02/Flower_ Garden.jpg

Page 33—Chris Rock photograph courtesy of: http://www. comedycentral.com/press/images/stand-up/chris-rock_kill-the-messenger.jpg

Page 34—Woman meditating photograph courtesy of: http://images. craveonline.com/article_imgs/Image/woman-doing-yoga-600.jpg

Page 35—Oprah Winfrey photograph courtesy of: http://www. adweek.com/adweek/photos/stylus/45921-OprahWinfrey.jpg

Page 37—Man on rock photograph courtesy of: http://rexburgoutdoors.com/outdoor1/headerimages/climb2.jpg

Page 41—Footprints in the sand photograph courtesy of: http://pondri.files.wordpress.com/2008/05/footprints_in_the_sand_op_493x600.jpg

Page 43—Graduation photograph courtesy of: http://www.buzzle.com/img/articleImages/320587-39530-44.jpg

Page 44—Two women talking photograph courtesy of: http://www.directsalesplr.com/Two%20Women%20Talking%20Over%20Coffee%20Resized.jpg

Page 50—Woman with light bulb photograph courtesy of: http://equintconsulting.com/wp-content/uploads/2008/10/istock_000005164183small.jpg

Page 53—Carlson Gracie, Jr. and Carlson Gracie, Sr. photograph courtesy of CrossOver Group: http://carlsongraciefederation.com/c1.jpg

Page 56—Concert photograph courtesy of: http://2.bp.blogspot.com/_mS8UxWB_9JE/ScMvAbVntqI/AAAAAAAABAA/PX1BkoriHZM/s400/concert_crowd.jpg

Page 58—Criss Angel walking on water photograph courtesy of: http://farm4.static.flickr.com/3168/2735753857_ecfbb7be7c.jpg?v=0

Page 59—Yacht photograph courtesy of: http://www.charterworld.com/images/yachts/Motor%20Yacht%20Jo%20-%20Cruising6.jpg

Page 61—Toddler reaching for stove photograph courtesy of: http://redcross.pmhclients.com/images/uploads/ST4K-BabyTouchingStove_thumb.jpg

Page 63—Man asleep on computer photograph courtesy of: http://teamowens313.files.wordpress.com/2008/11/insights_sleep_on_computer.jpg

Page 65—Maslow's Hierarchy of Needs illustration courtesy of: http://talkingtails.files.wordpress.com/2007/07/800px-maslows_hierarchy_of_needssvg.png

Page 67—Four food groups photograph courtesy of: http://behealthy.baystatebanner.com/issues/2009/0305/images/Four-food-groups.jpg

Page 68—Religious icons graphic courtesy of: http://boomeryearbook.com/blog/wp-content/uploads/2008/12/boomers-building-tolerance-understanding-people-of-different-religions.jpg

Page 69—Love image courtesy of: http://kunaljanu.files.wordpress.com/2009/02/thing-called-love.jpg

Page 70—Little superhero photograph courtesy of: http://www.life123.com/health/self-improvement/confidence/self-confidence-building.shtml

Page 71—Sunset meditation photograph courtesy of: http://www.padmakshiyoga.com/iStockYogaWomanMeditating.jpg

Page 77—New York magazine cover image courtesy of: http://www.easyvegan.info/img/madoff-monster.jpg

Page 78—You Have The Power image courtesy of: http://www1.eere.energy.gov/femp/images2/yhtp_cm_coreclr.jpg

Page 83—World Revolves Around Me image courtesy of: http://fc05.deviantart.net/fs43/f/2009/060/c/e/The_world_revolves_around_ME_by_Descyber.png

Page 86—Wherever You Go, There You Are image courtesy of: http://farm4.static.flickr.com/3421/3767681994_17906295e5_o.jpg

Page 89—Choice Exit Sign image courtesy of: http://marcelschwantescoaching.files.wordpress.com/2009/12/choice-sign.jpg

Page 91—Use Condoms WhipitOut Comedy image courtesy of: http://x51.xanga.com/35ff2a5037032242955670/z192447375.jpg

Page 92—Slow Down Sign photograph courtesy of: http://www.adaringadventure.com/blog/wordpress/wp-content/uploads/2009/01/slow-down-sign.jpg

Page 98—Canyon photograph courtesy of: http://www.planetside.co.uk/terragen/tgd/images/deep_canyon_v04.jpg

Page 99—Lips Shhh photograph courtesy of: http://www.dockwalk.com/uploadedImages/Dockwalk/Essentials/Hot_Topics/ShhStory.jpg

Page 105—Life Is Beautiful image courtesy of: http://media.photobucket.com/image/life%20is%20beautiful/Niccola111/life-is-beautiful.gif

Page 107—Pot of gold and rainbow image courtesy of: http://activerain.com/image_store/uploads/1/2/7/9/8/ar125209493889721.jpg

Page 108—Road and Sunset photograph courtesy of: http://www.thewallpapers.org/wallpapers/17/1712/thumb/320_2-Country-Road-Sunset.jpg

Page 118—Woman Holding Blank Tablet photograph courtesy of: http://jeanfranzblau.files.wordpress.com/2009/01/blank-slate1.jpg

Page 119—Rewind Button image courtesy of: http://media.scout.com/Media/Image/23/237748.jpg

Page 127—Crystal Ball image courtesy of: http://www.mediabistro.com/fishbowlny/original/crystal-ball%5B1%5D.jpg

Page 131—Jack Welch photograph courtesy of: http://www.ceowannabe.com/images/jackwelch.jpg

Page 133—General Electric logo image courtesy of: http://blog.tmcnet.com/beyond-voip/GE%20logo.jpg

Page 139—Six Sigma is a registered trademark of the Motorola Company.

Page 141—Woman Jumping Out of Water photograph: http://4.bp.blogspot.com/_pMOfeJwc6Ww/SK2YCePfvZI/AAAAAAAABCU/EGHHlQXFStY/s400/Leaping+Lady.jpg

Page 142—Cover of Jack Welch Straight From The Gut image courtesy of: http://images.51eng.com/products/JackStraightfromtheGut8_f.jpg

Page 145—Gold Bar Image courtesy of: http://www.fleseri.com/storage/say-no-to-gold.jpg

Page 147—Let Love Rule image courtesy of: http://hussainyousif.files.wordpress.com/2009/12/let-love-rule_-art-journaling.jpg

Page 149—Expect Nothing image courtesy of: http://img2.visualizeus.com/thumbs/09/05/05/graphic,design,typography-e8aeca91c0c630b26cae5bbdb5bb0c4c_h.jpg

Page 153—Passage of Time image courtesy of: http://img.brothersoft.com/screenshots/softimage/p/passage_of_time-29756-1229323568.jpeg

Page 154—Nielsen 4th quarter, 2009 A2/M2 Three Screen Report

Page 156—The Critic image courtesy of: http://www.bildango.com/wp-content/uploads/2009/12/jay_sherman_it_stinks.jpg

Page 159—Elmo plate image courtesy of: http://images.buycostumes.com/mgen/merchandiser/28658.jpg

Page 166—Curly from City Slickers photograph courtesy of: http://www.collider.com/uploads/imageGallery/City_Slickers/city_slickers_movie_image_jack_palance___1_.jpg

Page 168—Fry cook photograph courtesy of: http://www. blogcdn.com/jobs.aol.com/articles/media/2009/11/fast-food-cook-300raw112309.jpg

Page 174—Man laughing photograph courtesy of: http://cdn.edu-search.com/uploads/laugh.jpg

Page 177—Man in hard hat photograph courtesy of: http://www. betterphoto.com/uploads/processed/0017/0402290952501hardhat-020a.jpg

Page 184—Man with angel and devil cartoon courtesy of: durkinworks.blogspot.com/2008_04_01_archive.html

Page 187—YES! Image courtesy of: http://www.k-osmusic.com/images/yes_logo.png

Page 188—Woman jumping in air photograph courtesy of: http://www.freedomjumping.com/profiles/profile/show?id=DevonSwartz

Page 194—Café du Monde photograph courtesy of: http://media. photobucket.com/image/cafe%20du%20monde/ChaCha_Pepperoni/beignets-cafe-du-monde--large-msg-1.jpg

Page 195—Sean Rich with Pirates photograph courtesy of: http://www.tortugatrading.com/data/inspect.asp?Item=526&Filter=Movie+Memorabilia&Name=Sean+and+Pirates+on+set+at+Disney+Studios%2C+Burbank%2C+CA

Page 197—Coach John Wooden photograph courtesy of: http://2. bp.blogspot.com/_F5RpodBMz14/SxPReUq7rdI/AAAAAAAADdQ/IK15uZjIE54/s1600/JOHN+WOODEN4.jpg

Page 203—Parade Magazine cover courtesy of: http://tinypic.com/view.php?pic=30c9iqr&s=3

Page 208, 215, and 216—Coat of Arms template courtesy of: http://www.familyhistoryquickstart.com/2007/10/11/family-coat-of-arms/

Page 220—Hospital photo courtesy of: http://www.hospitalpuppet. com/Dorothy%20Chiles,%20Grandchildren,%20Death%20Bed.jpg

Page 225—Richard Branson photograph courtesy of: http://www.canonpalmer.redbridge.sch.uk/learning/businessstudies/RichardBransonVirgin.jpg

ABOUT THE AUTHOR

S teve Olsher has spent the last 20 years developing and refining the unique theories and exercises in this book.

Steve is a lifelong entrepreneur who has applied his street smarts, business acumen, and communication skills to a wide range of endeavors.

He has worked as a radio and nightclub DJ ("Mr. Bold"); owned his own nightclub at the age of 20 (The Funky Pickle!); developed a wine and spirits catalog business (Liquor by Wire); launched one of the Internet's first fully-functional e-commerce websites in 1995 (LiquorByWire.com); is the chairman and co-founder of San Francisco-based Liquor.com; is president and founder of Bold Development, one of Chicago's largest boutique real estate development companies; and is the founder and facilitator of The Reinvention Workshop.

Steve has earned the rank of purple belt in Brazilian Jiu-Jitsu, training under the late Carlson Gracie Sr. and now under Carlson Gracie Jr.

All of Steve's broad real-world experiences have contributed to the field-tested ideas in this book.

Steve lives in Chicago with his wife, Lena, and their three sons, Bobby, Isaiah and Xavier—who remind him every day why his motto is "Let Love Rule."

Breinigsville, PA USA
04 September 2010
244870BV00006B/4/P